To O...
Be...

SIDNEY FOX'S
CRIME

THE TRUE STORY OF
SIDNEY HARRY FOX AND
THE MARGATE MURDER

BY

GLENN CHANDLER

Grosvenor House
Publishing Limited

The right of Glenn Chandler to be identified as the author of this
work has been asserted in accordance with Section 78
of the Copyright, Designs and Patents Act 1988

The book cover picture is copyright to Jon Bradfield

This book is published by
Grosvenor House Publishing Ltd
28-30 High Street, Guildford, Surrey, GU1 3EL.
www.grosvenorhousepublishing.co.uk

A CIP record for this book
is available from the British Library

ISBN 978-1-80381-540-4
eBook ISBN 978-1-80381-541-1

Glenn Chandler is best known as the creator and writer of *Taggart*, which became the longest running detective series in the world. He has also written true crime television dramas, notably those on William Palmer the poisoner, George Joseph Smith the 'Brides in the Bath' killer, and John George Haigh, the acid bath murderer. His books include *Burning Poison*, a true account of a Georgian Liverpool murder mystery, and two fictional novels about Brighton detective Steve Madden, *Savage Tide* and *Dead Sight*. He is also an award-winning theatre writer, producer and director.

His last book, *The Sins of Jack Saul*, the true story of a rent boy from Dublin who became involved in two major Victorian scandals, ran to two editions and has sold across the world.

Dedicated to the memory of Alan John Clark
1943–2022

CONTENTS

PREFACE

31 August 1939

Crash!

With one word, the reporter for the *Isle of Thanet Advertiser* began his article on the demolition of the Metropole Hotel in Margate, for almost half a century a familiar seaside landmark on the north coast of Kent. It stood by the jetty, glory faded, facade worn, its reputation sealed by a murder only a decade earlier. The case had made it notorious, not only in Margate but throughout the country.

Now it was going, and while some were sorry to see it leave, others saw progress. The land was required for a new road. The Metropole was in the way. Like thousands of buildings, the hotel had seen its day, served its purpose. The rooms were tired, and the last people to have stayed there would not have mourned its passing. What lingered was the memory, sharpened by tongues over time, stirred in conversations, evoked in countless retellings over the years that sought to bring a conclusion to one question.

What did happen in Room 66?

Almost everyone was sure they knew or at least had their own theory. Besides, the participants were dead now, beyond telling, their souls gone to rest; one returned to dust in a Norfolk churchyard, the other hanged by the neck and buried in the grounds of Maidstone Prison. And now the bricks and mortar which might have told the story were passing on too. The night when a female guest died in dramatic and mysterious circumstances, her son later to be charged with her murder, was passing into folklore.

Sites of sensational murders gather about them a particular frisson. Some houses in which serial killers commit their dreadful crimes are demolished, as happened in the appalling cases of Ian Brady and Myra Hindley, and the Wests of Gloucester, whose Cromwell Street charnel house is now a pleasant garden. It is more difficult with flats, like the two London addresses where Dennis Nilsen dismembered his victims and flushed them down the toilet. Hotel rooms are in the same category. You can decorate and refurbish, but as long as the building remains, the space stays the same, contained within well-defined walls. There will always be a corridor leading to that room. There will always be that room and a door. That door.

It was said locally that no one wanted to book the room anyway, to sleep there, because of the unpleasant associations. But for ten years after the crime, there were inevitably those of a more ghoulish persuasion who were driven by curiosity. Guests wandered the first-floor corridor, asking for the room to be pointed out. Some visitors stayed in it without even knowing. What happened in Room 66 of the Metropole Hotel in Margate was not on a par with the aforementioned cases; the deed took only a few minutes, perhaps longer. But it led to one of the most controversial and unusual trials in English criminal history.

Roll back the years further to the final decade of the 1890s when Victoria was still on the throne. The hotel had only just risen from the ashes of the old Grand which had been destroyed by fire. With its handsome red-brick frontage, the new hotel graced the seafront of that popular Kentish watering hole. It boasted a hundred beds, and almost every room commanded a sea view. They were advertised as sumptuously decorated throughout by Messrs Edwards and Roberts of Wardour Street, London. Visitors could avail themselves of hydraulic lifts, and there was electric light in all the principal rooms. The enormous kitchen was presided over by a French chef, the culinary results of whose genius were sampled on the day of its opening by the great and the good of Margate. Glasses were raised, and a toast made to a hotel that now stood 'in the finest atmosphere of God's earth'.

Now that fine atmosphere was thick with dust. As the upper floors were demolished, passers-by looked up, as did our reporter from the *Advertiser*. They watched as the space once occupied by Room 66 was absorbed by the falling debris. In just a few moments, the wrecker's ball destroyed what was left of it. By the next day, the Metropole was gone. Eyes eventually turned across the channel, thoughts to the sombre gathering clouds of war. Soon the world would be thrust into a conflagration in which millions would die, and one miserable, sad death in a Margate hotel room would seem almost insignificant.

Yet at the time, the press had enjoyed a bonanza with the alliterative qualities of the three 'M's. Murder,

Metropole, Margate. Room 66 had a ring to it. Not 63 or 107, but 66. Like two-thirds of the number of the Great Beast in Revelation. Murder at the Metropole. The Margate Murder. The Mystery of Room 66.

Agatha Christie could not have arranged it better.

CHAPTER ONE

'MY MOTHER IS IN THERE!'

23 October 1929

Britain was at the tail-end of what would later be looked back on as the Roaring Twenties. The economic boom after the Great War had brought prosperity to many. An increasing number of people owned cars, possessed telephones, listened to the radio. Female suffrage was well under way. There were new freedoms and opportunities. Then, in the autumn of the final year came the Wall Street Crash. It brought to a shattering end a decade of hope, revival, and unbridled optimism.

The Metropole had seen better days too. In fact it had seen all of its best ones. Once, Victorian dowager duchesses, Edwardian gentlemen in light linen suits, and fashionable and giddy young women with money to spend and bathing costumes at the ready had occupied the lofty public rooms. Now there were mainly commercial travellers and those whose business brought them to the coast. There was still a grand feel about the place, but it was seedy. Still, the Metropole survived on its reputation as the place to stay in Merry Margate.

It was during October, as New York fell into chaos and the reverberations began to be felt around the world, that a commercial traveller called Samuel Douglas Hopkins, a former Royal Navy seaman, returned to the hotel from a night on the town. At about 11.40pm, he was sitting in the lounge, enjoying a drink, when a handsome young man, naked except for his shirt, came running down the stairs in a state of panic.

'Where is the boots? I believe there's a fire. Where is the boots?' he cried out.

Hopkins leapt to his feet and sped up a separate flight of stairs to find the person responsible for cleaning boots, fetching luggage, and doing other menial tasks around the hotel, but not usually putting out fires. There was no sign of the 'boots', so Hopkins ran to the billiard saloon where he quickly passed on the message. He then raced upstairs after the young man, with a number of people from the saloon following, and found himself in the first-floor corridor outside 67, the door of which was shut. The panic-stricken guest opened it, and Hopkins followed him in. The room was full of smoke. There was a connecting door to 66, which was also closed.

'My mother is in there,' the young man said.

It would never be firmly established who first opened the connecting door to Room 66. There is no question, however, about the quantity of smoke. It was so thick that Hopkins was at first beaten back by it. He made a second attempt with a handkerchief pressed over his mouth but did not get much further. He could not see a thing. He went down on his hands and knees and crawled forward until he came into contact with the woman's legs. They were hanging over the edge of the bed. He managed to get his hands under her arms and pulled her down onto the floor. She was wearing nothing but a vest. When questioned, Hopkins could not recall whether she was actually in the bed or just lying on top of it, though it was clear she was lying aslant, with her head to the top and her feet to the bottom.

By this time, there were others in the room and outside in the corridor, most of them commercial travellers. One, Reginald Reed, was just visible to Hopkins through the pungent smoke and the glare. Hopkins begged for his assistance, and they pulled the woman out through the connecting door into the passageway. Reed went back into the room and discovered the source of the smoke, a large, upholstered armchair near the gas fire, which was smouldering heavily. He dragged that out into the corridor too, where a number of people threw glasses of water over it. A traveller called William Underwood and a sales engineer, Frederick George French, entered the room and observed that the gas fire was still on and that there were flames coming from the carpet where the chair had been. French stamped out the flames, turned off the gas, and threw open the window.

Another commercial traveller, Henry Miller, helped to carry the woman further along the corridor. He looked at her face and reckoned she was dead, as her mouth was open and she seemed to have no control over her muscles. By this time Police Constable George Edward Bray from the Margate Borough Police had arrived. He and four others carried the woman down to the lobby, away from the polluted air on that floor. They placed her at the foot of the stairs, where Bray used the Schafer method of artificial respiration by rolling her gently onto her right side, then onto her stomach and applying rhythmic pressure to the lower part of her thorax. He attempted about seventy-five movements but to no avail.

They observed there were no teeth in her mouth. In fact, her dentures, a complete set of upper and lowers, were found in the wash-hand basin in her room, suggesting she had gone to bed before the fire started. When the smoke cleared, Bray and his colleague, Sergeant Herbert Fleet, found her dress hanging up behind the door, her shoes under the bed, and her stockings hanging over the rail.

There was no money, luggage or jewellery of any description found in either room. Yet the couple had stayed there since 16 October. Initially the son had taken rooms for just one night, but four days later, their rooms were changed to 66 and 67 because his mother felt cold, and 66 had a gas fire. They had remained in these rooms until the 23rd, a period of seven days. The bill was £12.

The travellers who helped that night had tales to tell for long afterwards, and the plucky Hopkins suffered from the effects of smoke inhalation for about three weeks. He would later be awarded a certificate from the Society for the Protection of Life from Fire by the Mayor of Margate. But none of the guests who helped put out the fire and carry the woman downstairs were aware at the time of any circumstances other than that a distraught guest had lost his mother in a terrible accident.

The first medical man on the scene, Dr Austen, pronounced her dead from shock and suffocation. By the time the Margate Fire Brigade arrived, in the persons of Chief Officer Harry Hammond and his men along with tender and pump, the fire had been extinguished, and most of the smoke had escaped through the open window. Hammond, with his fire chief's eye for such things, noted that the seat of the fire was unquestionably beneath where the armchair had been, as the greatest damage was done to the carpet and the underside of the chair. There was a 'bridge' of unburnt carpet between the gas fire and the burned area.

When Inspector Palmer of the Margate Police questioned the guest at the centre of the tragedy, the dead woman's son became lucid and voluble. He gave his version of the events. He had lit the gas fire, gone downstairs to the bar for a drink, come back at about quarter to ten and gone to sleep in his own room. At around half past eleven, he heard his window rattling and smelt smoke. He went into his mother's room and was beaten back by it, just as Hopkins had been. He then ran downstairs for help. He told Palmer that all of his brothers had been killed in the war and that he had recently taken his mother across the channel to Belgium and France to see their graves in a cemetery near Arras.

Returning to the events of that evening, and conscious that the bill was still outstanding, he said that her handbag had contained twenty-four pounds as he had cashed a cheque for her the previous day. Inspector Palmer searched the handbag but it was empty. The couple, seemingly, had no clothes other than those on their backs. Yet no suspicion seemed to have been aroused, or if it was, it was cast aside. The distraught son, comforted by the hotel manager's wife, Mrs Harding, was given another room for the night.

The next day, the inquest jury returned a verdict of death by misadventure, and the funeral was hastily arranged in the Norfolk village from which the couple hailed. The burial took place six days later. Was it perhaps revulsion at the thought that a son could kill his mother which stopped people from questioning some of the strange features about that evening? For there was a background to the case as thick and impenetrable as the smoke which had filled Room 66, a dense black wall to all but a few. There were people who knew this couple, who knew the young man in particular, for whom there were many sparks of light in the darkness.

The son's name was Sidney Harry Fox. He was a confidence trickster, an impostor, a habitual and pathological liar, and a crook. He was also homosexual and a male prostitute who had been selling his body since he was a young teenager employed in fine houses as a page boy. His preference for men seemed to cause him no anxiety, in spite of sex between males then being illegal and carrying long prison sentences. At the same time, he was a devoted son, worshipped by his mother who herself, despite her walking stick and unsteadiness on her feet, was no paragon of virtue. (1)

In so many murder cases, the victim pales into insignificance. Not so Rosaline Fox. The story of Sidney Harry Fox and his mother, Rosaline, is unique in the annals of crime. Mrs Fox glows like a hot ember in this story, never fading, her bright cherubic face shining through the gloom.

To understand what brought this strange, devoted couple to Margate in 1929, one needs to travel back once more to before the turn of the century, step aboard the East Anglian railway, and alight at a small rural halt

between the towns of East Dereham and Swaffham
called Great Fransham.

* * * * * *

Chapter Note

1. While the word gay had a different meaning then, I have
taken the liberty of using it at times to describe Sidney's
lifestyle and his friends. I have also taken the liberty of
spelling his name Sidney instead of Sydney. It was good
enough for the report of his trial in the *Notable British Trials*
series and has been spelt both ways in contemporary reports
and in articles over the decades. It also avoids confusion with
the occasional references to Sydney, Australia.

CHAPTER TWO

GREAT FRANSHAM

Railways have a particular place in the story of Sidney and Rosaline Fox. It was the railway that opened up the eastern side of England, and brought from Doncaster to Norfolk the man who would become Rosaline Fox's husband. It was the railway that employed him as a signalman and the railway that took him away again out of her life. It was the railway that employed the man who would become Sidney Fox's father and the railway that eventually took the family away from Great Fransham to the smoke of London. And it was the railway which, in the end, took mother and son on innumerable journeys around the south of England. The railway provides the very arteries of the story. In the beginning, when Great Fransham, Little Fransham and neighbouring Necton were nothing but dirty, isolated and backward Norfolk hamlets, it was the Lynn and Dereham Railway, later to become part of the East Anglian, that delivered them into the nineteenth century.

Rosaline Rallison, as she started life, was born on 23 May 1866, the daughter of an agricultural labourer James Rallison and his wife, Maria, and the younger by seven years of two sisters. The extended family of Rallisons had not moved from the area. Three tiny cottages stood crammed side by side in the village, occupied by three Rallison brothers and their families, so Rosaline had no shortage of cousins, both male and female, with which to play. There were two older cousins a short distance away in the slightly larger community of Necton, and to visit them she would either walk or hitch up her skirt and plant herself on the back of a pony cart, perhaps that which belonged to her aunt in Chantry Lane who regularly made the journey between the two villages. Emma and Rose, her aunt's daughters on her mother's side, were newly married, Emma to the local blacksmith and Anna to a farmer, and were old enough to be guiding influences on their young cousin.

Chantry Lane in Necton was a road Rosaline would get to know well on her visits. It was little more than a rutted track on which lived the local thatcher, James Nelson, and his large family. Nelson was, and is, a not uncommon name in Norfolk, and the Chantry Lane Nelsons were only one of many local families who bore that famous sea-faring name. One of his sons, also called James, was ten years older than Rosaline and a boy who, while they may not have been childhood sweethearts, would remain in touch and much later play a very important part in her life.

This was the world in which Rosaline was raised, one of farmers, agricultural workers, shepherds, blacksmiths, bricklayers, thatchers and carters, along with the now ever-present railway and its invading army of porters, signalmen, footplate men and drivers. Far from being a quiet rural idyll, the countryside resounded to the sound of the hammer, the grinding of traction and the belching of steam.

In time, Rosaline's home village would boast three famous sons. William Crane, who set up the blacksmith's shop in the village, founded a company to manufacture field ambulances for the army. Vincent Raven, later Sir Vincent Raven, the son of the rector, would become Superintendent of the Royal Arsenal at Woolwich, in charge of organising munitions production. Rosaline would supply the third.

She grew to be a buxom and striking girl with many admirers among the local lads, so much so that villagers years hence would remember her as the village belle. Contemporary accounts describe her as unable to read or write, for schooling was basic at that time, and illiteracy was common in country districts. She seems to have kept herself pure, however, until her marriage to William George Fox in July 1887, when she was just over twenty-one. He was the same age. His parents had originally lived in Norfolk but had moved to Doncaster before he was born. By the time of their marriage, William Fox had uprooted and gone back down the line to Norfolk and was working with the railway as a porter.

He moved around the district and along the line, and Rosaline went with him. Their first child William was born just over nine months later in Harleston, and by the birth of their second son Reginald in Carlton Colville, just over the border into Suffolk, things were already not going well for them. It was not a happy marriage, and Rosaline was not a faithful wife. She went back to live on numerous occasions with her parents in Great Fransham, and by the time of the birth of their third son, Cecil Rallison Fox in 1894, they had fallen on hard times, for the boy was born in the Union Workhouse. Although William, or Billy Fox as he was popularly known around the area, dutifully signed the birth certificate, he was not Cecil's father. He had been promoted to signalman, but sadly all the signs were that the marriage was beyond saving. They were already having difficulty feeding and bringing up two sons, and now another baby was on the way.

Shortly after Cecil's birth, Billy Fox vanished out of Rosaline's life. A warrant was issued for his desertion, but Billy Fox was never traced. Trains brought the ability to disappear very quickly from one end of the country to another. Left without a breadwinner, Rosaline sank into dire poverty, existing on 4/6d (22.5p) parish relief and what little she could earn as a monthly nurse around the village. Monthly nurses remained with mothers for four weeks after they had given birth, providing what we would now call post-natal care; her lack of training compensated for by having nurtured three babies of her own.

Her life was soon to take another turn. At Great Fransham, the foreman in charge of the station was one Thomas Newell. He became Rosaline's lover and was, according to her eldest son, also Cecil's father. But there was a small problem on the line. He already had a wife and family in the village.

It was said of Rosaline Fox in those years that there was an 'air of mystery' about her and that she appeared to have a private income. It is hard to see how a married woman with three children on parish relief could convey the appearance of having any kind of private income unless it was a tactful way of saying she was kept by men. In later years, living in London, she would not be short of gentleman callers. Whatever the circumstances, Thomas Newell became the father of her fourth child, born on 2 Jan 1899. She called him Sidney Harry Fox.

Sidney's birth certificate is the only one on which the space for the father's name is blank. Sidney's paternity was no secret in the village, and Newell was obliged to pay Rosaline a weekly sum for the boy's upkeep. Rosaline and her aged father, James Rallison, and her four sons now lived together in a small labourer's cottage a walk across the field from the village church of All Saints and Great Fransham school, the primitive little building to which she had gone as a girl, and the one at which Sidney and all his brothers would now be educated.

Sidney, when he grew up, would claim that his illegitimacy didn't bother him, that he knew about it from an early age, and that all he ever wanted was for his mother to be happy. It was however a major stigma at the time. Thomas Newell's legitimate son, Walter, who was Sidney's half-brother and just a year older, attended the same village school. Cecil's illegitimacy wasn't so well known, as both Billy Fox and Thomas Newell had still been around, and Billy Fox had put his name to the birth certificate despite knowing he was not Cecil's father. Reginald and William, the legitimate sons, never had to endure the word bastard being applied to them as it must have been to Sidney. It was something Sidney would have to carry through life.

While it may not have bothered him at first, it was a burden that would greatly affect his character.

The school was built to accommodate eighty pupils, but by the time Sidney was admitted the number was only thirty-eight. Today, the building, which still stands in the corner of a field and serves as a village hall, looks as though it scarcely could have held even that. Records survive that describe it in various reports as dark and in need of new equipment and more windows. There was no fireguard or clock, the maps were torn, and the place was frequently dusty and cold, as the fire was not always lit before the children assembled. When it was, the chimney billowed smoke into the classroom. There was no playground, and the children had to play in the road, which would not, of course, be quite so dangerous as today. Teaching at the school was described as ineffective. When the class rose to sing, it was a dreadful cacophony, while of grammar the pupils knew very little. Discipline was also hard to maintain. A lot of children at Great Fransham were reported as being very backward for their age, one boy, Willie Burton, being excluded for being 'a great deal of trouble and mentally deficient'.

Regular outbreaks of scarlet fever, typhoid and whooping cough occurred which shut it down for periods, but when the children were able to attend there were frequent absences because parents, who were mostly agricultural workers and farmers, kept them behind to work on the land. There existed considerable resentment in country districts to the Elementary Education Act of 1880, which insisted on compulsory attendance from five to ten years. Instead of working to bring in money, they had to spend their days cooped up in classrooms learning nothing useful. By the time Sidney went to school, it had been raised to twelve.

On the plus side, it was a school where, if you were at least bright and applied yourself, you might come out ready to make your way in the world. Sidney Fox did just that. He sat for his labour certificate, passed, and on 16 May walked out of the school, a twelve-year-old able to read and write, add up figures and pronounce himself fit to get a job. But what was there to do with his education in Great Fransham? He struck on an idea. He would collect for charity. He armed himself with a collecting tin and a notebook and set off from house to house in the district, this bright-eyed Robin Hood with his plan to redistribute wealth. Which charity is unknown, though it turned out it began at home.

He appropriated for himself about fifteen shillings of the money and covered it up by gumming two pages of the book together, so the donations which amounted to that sum couldn't be traced. It might have been better to have simply not recorded the donations at all if that had been possible, for when it was discovered that one of the pages in the book was thicker than the others, his scam was unmasked. For this, he was taken to the local police station and birched. Sidney had just committed his first fraud.

If it wasn't clear then, it was obvious soon afterwards that Great Fransham was too small a place for a boy of Sidney's talents. William had already fled the family nest, abandoning his trade as a bricklayer, and joined the Norfolk Regiment. Reginald and Cecil were working as farm labourers, and if war hadn't broken out, they might well have carried on in that capacity, just as their grandfather had all his life and his generation before him. But the call to arms mobilised families across the country. Cecil followed his brother into the Norfolk Regiment while, at the age of fifteen, too young to join up and more attracted by the glamour of town life, Sidney upped sticks and took the train to London to look for a situation. Rosaline followed soon afterwards.

She and Reginald took a small Victorian terraced house in Thornton Heath near Croydon, but Rosaline had her sights set on better. With her nursing experience, she applied to help the Red Cross. Reginald, registered unfit for the army, found a job helping the war effort at the Woolwich Arsenal munitions factory. Rosaline may have been relieved not to lose another son overseas, but there were dangers at home she was unprepared for.

It took an upheaval like the war to remove a close-knit rural family like the Foxes from the land and tear them asunder. The early years of fighting would do more than separate them; it would devastate them. Her youngest, Sidney, had demonstrated an early propensity for crime, and while Rosaline hoped a steady job might keep him out of trouble, the bright lights of the capital were too big a draw not to provide him with further opportunities. Adventure awaited. He would take full advantage of them.

* * * * * *

CHAPTER THREE

ADVENTURES OF A PAGE BOY

Sidney's feelings on arrival in the big city were summed up in 'My Life Story', a potted and vainglorious account he wrote for the *News of the World* when the bright lights had all been put out for him.

'The call of towns and cities and life beyond Great Fransham came to me early and never departed. I still love town life, the glamour of the West End, its gay lights and its never-ceasing whirl. I know something too of the tragedies behind the glamour, and the disillusionment behind the lights. Others knew it before me; others have yet to learn. There are "good time men" as well as "good time girls" and I regret to say I turned out eventually to be one of the former.'

If there was a hint of his burgeoning sexuality and growing interest in the male sex in this, it was the only one. His account was self-serving and less than truthful, leaving out much that he didn't want to be remembered for. The good time man was then still barely fifteen, and at loose in a city of over two million people. But first he had to find a job. He landed his first as a page boy in the household of Mrs Gertrude Hargreaves of Leamington, Stone Grove, Edgware. A northern suburb, it didn't quite boast the seductive lights of the West End, but those were only a short train ride away.

His stay with Mrs Hargreaves was a minor stop on his journey and didn't feature in his story, but it reveals a great deal about his developing character.

While Mrs Hargreaves was away, she left the house in charge of the cook, during which time a number of ostrich feathers and underclothes, valued at about five pounds, went missing. Suspicion fell on a twenty-two-year-old nursery governess, Florence Hall, who was charged with stealing them. Sidney had become quite friendly with Florence and lent her some money, or so he said, but their friendship was to end abruptly. He informed Mrs Hargreaves on her return that he had seen the governess wrapping up the items, and that she had given them to him in a parcel to post.

By this time Miss Hall had left and gone back to her home in Nottingham, unaware that her reputation had been maligned. Mrs Hargreaves wrote to her and demanded that she return the items. Thefts by servants, even of small items, were taken very seriously. Miss Hall tore up the letter, which she said was in rude terms, and returned it, threatening to sue for libel. A warrant was issued for her arrest, and she was brought back to London and put before the magistrates. She denied vehemently ever taking the underwear (the ostrich feathers were dropped from the proceedings) and called Fox the page boy spiteful, claiming that it was all lies. She denied returning to Nottingham because of any criminality on her part and said it was because she didn't feel comfortable, and that there was not enough food at Mrs Hargreaves.

Sidney took the stand, his first appearance in a courtroom. He said the defendant had never complained about the food, and that he had admonished her when he saw her taking the items.

'They belong to Mrs Hargreaves, you had better leave them alone,' he said, to which she replied, 'Mind your own business.'

She told him if she could get hold of some money she would go home, and the following morning she obtained five pounds, and Sidney lent her another few shillings. He helped her get her luggage ready and went with her to St Pancras. She said to him, 'I don't think I shall see you any more.' She then caught the train to Nottingham.

Her defence solicitor Mr Robinson addressed the bench and asked them to think twice before sending the defendant for trial, pointing out that the case rested largely upon the evidence of 'the lad Fox'. It was of such a flimsy character, he said, that he felt convinced no jury would convict on it. The magistrates agreed and the case was dismissed. What happened was never established, and the undergarments were never found, though it was almost certain Sidney was the thief. Soon after, 'the lad Fox' left Mrs Hargreaves' employment. It wasn't the first time he would attempt to apportion blame on others, as would soon be demonstrated.

He quickly found another position, once more as a page boy, this time in a much more illustrious household. He was a blue-eyed, fresh-faced, very pretty young man, who had already discovered his abilities to turn heads and take advantage of his innocent good looks. He would use this to his ultimate advantage at the home of

Sir John and Lady Constance Leslie of Manchester Square in Marylebone.

Lady Constance was one of society's grand dames. Her mother was alleged to be the daughter of George IV and Mrs Fitzherbert, so it could be said that Sidney came to work for royalty, albeit from the wrong side of the blanket. Lady Constance was eighty-six years old and 'the last source of much of the forgotten talk and high society gossip of Victorian times'. Born in the same year the Queen came to the throne, she appeared to have known everybody who was anybody throughout the second half of the last century. Her husband, who was ninety-two, was a baronet with a distinguished military career behind him and a patron in art and literary circles. They entertained on a massive scale at both their London and County Monaghan residences in Ireland, one of which was the magnificent Castle Leslie. As host and hostess, the Leslies had few equals in society for their balls and dinner parties, their doors open to prime ministers, members of the House of Lords, famous painters, musicians and sportsmen. It was this wealthy, deeply conservative and autocratic pair of socialites for whom Sidney Fox now took up employment.

'Even now I recall how awed I was when I got out in the whirl of traffic to make my way to Manchester Square,' he wrote. 'It was during my service here with those kindly gentle people that I grew familiar with luxury. I, a country bumpkin from Great Fransham!'

Kindly and gentle they may have been, but by the time Sidney arrived, Lady Constance could no longer stand the sight of her husband and had designed a large floral table ornament, reputedly so she would not have to look at him over dinner. None of this affected Sidney, who saw only wealth and opulence and, above all, class.

For the grandson of an agricultural labourer and a railway foreman's son to be opening the door to titled gents and ladies was something Rosaline could only have dreamed about in their spartan Norfolk cottage. And how utterly perfect he looked in his page boy uniform. The Leslies took to him straight away and very soon regarded him as the family pet. They even gave him a nickname. They called him Cupid.

The Leslies' daughter, Lady Theodosia Bagot, also saw much to adore in the perfect young servant. Dosia to the family, she was married to Colonel Sir Josceline Fitzroy Bagot, a British army officer and Conservative politician. Like her elderly parents, Lady Bagot could see nothing amiss behind the lad's handsome face and polite manners. She took a great interest in him. Sidney did not exaggerate when he marvelled how a mere country bumpkin could land on such fertile soil.

His duties were mainly to look after the increasingly frail Sir John, with whom he developed a close bond. One of his tasks was to take the old gentleman for his morning walk, and he would often be seen helping him around the square. Ambassadors, their wives and the social elite occupied much of Manchester Square, and Sir John would stop on occasion and talk to them as they enquired after his health.

It gave Sidney many an opportunity to watch how the upper classes behaved, an education he could never have received at Great Fransham village school. It would stand him in good stead. On his days off, he wandered into the West End of London, looking into grand shops and at the beautifully dressed women—and undoubtedly men too—who patronised them. He discovered dance halls, theatres and music halls. He was on the cusp of a life he could never have imagined himself living.

Though the Leslies adored him, his fellow servants were not so enamoured. As in his previous post in Edgware, when things went wrong, he always threw the blame on them, but with such a cherubic gaze that he was given the benefit of the doubt. A pattern was firmly set.

His tastes, now he had turned sixteen, were much too expensive for his wages. He stole some silver from his new employers. It was also reported he even made overtures to an elderly housemaid and embezzled her, though details are now hard to come by. The Leslies eventually had to let him go but were loath to prosecute. They simply could not bear the knowledge that the charming boy they had taken under their wing was a thief and a fraudster. On top of that, there was his young age to consider.

There is a tendency to think that homosexual men of the era had enough problems to contend with. The ever-present threat of prosecution and blackmail were quite enough without adding the risks of being caught and imprisoned for theft and fraud. Sidney was in no way deterred from any of them. It was all criminality at the end of the day, and if you were going to be sent to prison for being yourself, you might as well take all that was on offer. There is little doubt that while working as a page boy, Sidney learned to use his sexuality to fund the lifestyle that he saw others enjoying. In that he was no different from many young men who had arrived in the capital before him, and many who would come after.

In a number of ways his trajectory was similar to that of Jack Saul, a rent boy from Dublin who, in the 1880s, came to London and was attracted to the rich and the aristocratic. Jack had also been a servant in a fine house and had committed thefts. He slept with titled gentlemen. He was attracted to men in uniform (as Sidney was too, as we shall see), and he flouted the law with abandon. Jack also made the most of his looks, at least while they lasted. Both had mothers whom they ultimately supported. (1)

The years after the Great War were very different from the Victorian London of Jack Saul. Millions of men had been thrust together away from home, and blackout London had become a place of excitement and adventure for those in search of sex and more. There were still dangers, but what were those compared to the four years of hell the country had endured?

By the age of sixteen, Sidney would be involved with a man whose courting of danger was off the scale.

* * * * * *

Chapter Note

1. See the author's *The Sins of Jack Saul* (Grosvenor House Publishing)

CHAPTER FOUR

A DANGEROUS
MAN TO KNOW

Gerald Hamilton possessed a fondness for page boys. The twenty-six-year-old *bon vivant* had recently returned from a tour of Europe, during which he visited the lavish Royal Palace at Dresden where he 'almost fainted at the sight of good-looking page boys in their teens, the flowers of the Saxon aristocracy, in their brilliant and uncomfortable cornflower-blue uniforms' as he would describe them in one of his own grossly unreliable autobiographies. He also had a fetish for scarlet-uniformed guardsmen from the Household Cavalry whom he picked up in London, at places such as the Covent Garden Hotel and public houses on the Edgware Road, and paid to flog him at his plush flat in Westminster.

Sidney described him simply but proudly as the greatest fraudster known to Scotland Yard. He claimed to have met Hamilton when he was in Brixton Prison, but declined to name him as he was then no longer inside. In fact, Sidney met him before either of them would ever go to prison, probably in one of the pubs he frequented while exploring the West End and beyond. London, during the Great War years, had a sizeable underground, and sometimes not so underground, gay scene. Sidney's description of his friend as the greatest fraudster known to the police was no exaggeration. Gerald Hamilton was at the start of his own long road to notoriety.

He would in time befriend Christopher Isherwood and become famous as the character inspiration for the sexual masochist Mr Norris in *Mr Norris Changes Trains*. He had no such claim to literary fame when he met Sidney, but he was already known to the police in London as a 'notorious sodomite'.

Born in Shanghai as Gerald Frank Hamilton Souter, where his father had been an agent for a Chinese merchant firm, he was packed off to England at two months old to be brought up in the care of a maiden aunt. He first went to a prep school in Berkshire, where he was bullied mercilessly for his effeminacy, but seemed to enjoy it, then to Rugby. There, as an adolescent and sexually precocious schoolboy, he was initiated into the normal homosexual practises that went on in such institutions, fuelled by the regime of sixth-form prefects who beat lower boys on their bottoms with canes or long-handled clothes brushes. This was how, in all likelihood, Gerald developed his taste for chastisement, just like Mr Norris in Isherwood's novel. Eventually, he was caught in bed with another boy and asked to leave for the good of the school.

By his early twenties, Gerald was already living an eccentric and bohemian lifestyle. He came to the notice of the trenchant and traditionally conservative magazine, *John Bull,* as one of the guests at a 'bohemian ball' in Pelham Street, Chelsea, held by Sir Frederick Williams, described as a 'sprig of aristocracy'. In reality, Williams was a young, gay and wealthy baronet from Cornwall, while Gerald was more than just a guest. A representative of the magazine obtained a ticket, and discovered within its dimly lit rooms a three-foot figure of Christ standing upright in a coffin lined with black velvet, a hideous human skull 'guarded by incense', and, horror of horrors, a framed photograph of Oscar Wilde. The magazine did not 'think it necessary' to comment in any detail upon Sir Frederick's abnormal tastes. With such an account, it had a already done a fine job.

Gerald's first run-in with the police, or at least the French police, was when he shared a villa in Dieppe the following year with his aristocratic young sprig of a lover. The pair had been assaulted by two French youths while walking home, and Gerald reported them. The attack was clearly not random. Sir Frederick and Gerald, who was tactfully described as the aristocrat's 'boy friend', were found to be sharing the villa with five English youths they had brought over on holiday. *John Bull* was still on the case, and clearly had its teeth sharpened for what they called 'The South Kensington Gang'. They described the goings-on in the French villa as disgusting orgies. Gerald's nickname was Miss Violet, while 'he and others of the boys dressed themselves as girls, painted their lips and cheeks, called each other "dears" and "loves", indulged in extravagant kissing, and generally acted in an unnatural manner'. When the French youths came to trial, one was also charged with committing unnatural offences with Gerald. The two quickly returned to London.

There, Gerald set himself up in a bachelor establishment with two exotic Chinese servants, Ah Sung and Kwai Ching, the former of which would glide around the flat posing in front of mirrors in silk dressing gowns. He became a Catholic, something which infuriated his father and drove a wedge between them, just one more example of his reluctance to conform to what anyone or society expected of him. An obsessive European traveller who rarely stayed at home for very long periods, Gerald introduced and ingratiated himself wherever he went. On his latest sexual pilgrimage, he had taken time off to have a private audience with the Pope, kiss the ring of St Peter, and use his contacts to mix and socialise with the Catholic aristocracy. He also made many German friends, most but not all of whom he would lose contact with at the outbreak of war, something he deeply resented. While in Europe, he blew his inheritance at the rate of about ten thousand a year, an enormous sum to expend at that time.

Invited back to his new friend's first-floor apartment at Dacre House, just off Victoria Street, Sidney's eyes must have watered at the interior decor and how Gerald had achieved so much. Gerald had, of course, achieved nothing himself, except a reputation. His study and bedroom, which he referred to as the Chinese Room, had black walls and a yellow ceiling, while the dining room was furnished with Chinese Chippendale. Treasures on display included valuable pieces of oriental lacquerware such as a tree trunk with the sitting figure of the Goddess Kwan Yin, a stunning red fruit bowl made partly of silk which had taken years to make by hand, and a figure representing the Goddess of Mercy. They weren't actually his but those of a gallery owner for whom he was storing them. Gerald was not beyond boasting to guests that they belonged to him.

For a country boy desperate to experience the naughtier side of London, Sidney could have no greater teacher than Gerald Hamilton. And Gerald could have no prettier companion and student than Sidney. The influence Gerald Hamilton had over the boy from Norfolk should not be underestimated. Although he knew some glamorous and well-connected people, it wasn't enough for him. Neither was one biography. They all, infuriatingly for biographers, gave different accounts of the same events. Gerald was a spinner of yarns, a liar and a fantasist who told marvellous stories about himself. He claimed to have known Roger Casement, the Irish revolutionary who was later hanged, a story dismissed by many as nothing but fantasy. He would boast of meeting Rasputin while on a trip to Russia, another unlikely tale. The man who would become Isherwood's Mr Norris would document his life in such a way that made it impossible to completely separate fact from fiction. Probably Gerald couldn't either. As we shall see, Sidney would take after him.

The police files, on the other hand, can be relied upon. Sidney and Gerald soon became intimate, and Gerald began writing letters to him in less than careful language and sending them to his mother's house. Sidney enjoyed writing letters too. At least Gerald had the wisdom to address his from an accommodation address, a block of exclusive bachelor chambers just off St James in Park Place where he rented a room. Sidney lacked the wisdom to destroy the letters and kept them. It was clear he worshipped Gerald. His new friend appeared to know everyone who was worth knowing, so it is tempting to wonder if he took the sixteen-year-old budding fraudster to the Cafe Royal, where he was—genuinely—well in with what remained of the old Oscar Wilde set, Lord Alfred Douglas and Robert Ross.

Had Sidney possessed a fortune, it would have made him even more attractive than he was. Gerald Hamilton had a well-earned reputation for separating friends and colleagues from their bank accounts. He also had a coterie of very dodgy acquaintances.

Another of the old Wilde set was Maurice Schwabe, who changed his name to Shaw in 1911 when the police got too near to his criminal activities. It was Schwabe who, having slept with Oscar Wilde, originally introduced the playwright to Alfred Taylor, in whose flat Wilde met the young men who would be his downfall. Schwabe had also been a lover of Lord Alfred Douglas, who wrote a long series of passionate letters to him addressed 'Darling Pretty Boy', signing himself off with expressions like 'your loving boy-wife'. Schwabe, or Shaw as he now was, had long lost his pretty boy looks. Like the fictional Dorian Gray, but without a painting in the attic to bear the marks of his passage through life, he was now in his mid-forties, and part of an international ring of card-sharpers. He sold shares in dubious business enterprises, and sought out young men with the aim of separating them from their inheritances. While Gerald enjoyed his sexual pleasures with Sidney, he and Maurice Shaw were in league, engaged in defrauding a second young man of his considerable fortune.

Archibald Walker was the fresh-faced, good-looking son of a wealthy wool merchant who, at twenty-one, had come into his parents' marriage settlement of thirty-thousand pounds. Within a few years it was gone, siphoned of into a partnership which traded as Walker Shaw Syndicate, but which did not actually do very much if anything at all. If Sidney needed any lessons from the big league in divesting people of money, he need not have looked much further than Gerald Hamilton and Maurice Shaw, the latter now posing as a financier and company promoter. It seems the company actually had an office, for there was at least one acrimonious exchange there. (1)

When Maurice was killed in the war, his estate was valued at less than five hundred pounds. Walker, then bankrupt, would claim, 'well at least I will get something back'. A fool and his money is a term that comes easily to mind. A plucked pigeon was the phrase used in the bankruptcy court.

Sidney had nothing worth plucking except his youth, but it is interesting to speculate how much he modelled himself on his new acquaintances. Sidney was impressionable. As a page boy he had opened the doors to aristocracy, and practised the patter of their class because he knew it would open doors for him. Now he was with outright scoundrels, who seemed to be doing very well out of their business. Against such men, his charity-book fraud and his page boy thefts looked like small potatoes.

What Sidney didn't know as he made his way home to his mother, probably just as well for him, was that his new and exciting friend was being tailed by Special Branch detectives. Neither did Gerald. He had come back from Europe, ostensibly to arrange with his bankers to have money sent to him abroad, but it was already known to Special Branch that one of Gerald's friends was the shabby financier Albert Edward Heyr, who at the start of the war had conned dozens of people into investing in bizarre schemes involving diamonds from South Africa. Gerald was also intimate with Rudolf Stallman, alias the Baron von Koenig, alias the Baron von Rossbach, alias Rudolph Lemoine, a German criminal and fugitive from justice who had connections with German intelligence. They had been on a motoring holiday through Bavaria together, and Stallman had helped Gerald obtain invitations to parties and receptions at the German Embassy.

All of this added up to only one thing. Gerald Hamilton was a security threat.

Rosaline, meanwhile, had enough distractions without having to worry about what her youngest was doing on his nights out in London and with whom he was keeping company. One of them was a happy diversion, the other tragic.

Sidney's eldest brother William had been shipped out to India with his regiment but was sent home with a shattered knee. No longer able to take part in active service, he took a job as a tram conductor in Croydon. It was very likely while collecting fares that he started talking to one of his passengers, a builder's daughter called Lily Elizabeth Bish. They were married on 12 July 1915 at Christ Church, Croydon, where Sidney signed the register as a witness. The following year they had a daughter, the only child of their marriage. They called her Marjorie Maria Rosaline Fox. She was destined to become Rosaline's only grandchild. They set up their own home in Epsom, but it wasn't long before William found a new job, that of a male nurse at a hospital in Ewell.

On 14 November that same year, Reginald Fox was killed when a fragment from the exploding fuse of a shell lacerated his colon and right ureter. He died of the injuries in the Royal Arsenal Hospital. Working with ammunition was dangerous. Sidney told the story that his brother died in the Woolwich Arsenal explosion earlier that year when three men were injured, possibly because it was a better documented incident and sounded more dramatic. Reginald was buried at the Queens Road Cemetery in Croydon. His coffin bore a brass breast-plate bearing his full name Reginald Mitchell Fox. He was twenty-four.

After her son's death, Rosaline decided it was time to move house. On a trip home to Norfolk, she met an old acquaintance who introduced her to her son, Henry Rix, an old boy of Swaffham Grammar School. Rix was on holiday from London, where he had been for some years, and working in a well-paid job as a merchant's ledger clerk. At that time, he was living in a furnished flat at 26 Cavendish Mansions in Hampstead and thinking of joining the navy. He was looking for someone to take over the flat while he was away. Rosaline mentioned that she had always wanted to live in the Hampstead district. With an astonishing disregard for the truth, which shows that Rosaline was very much the block from which Sidney had been chipped, she told Rix that Sidney had also been an old boy of the same school. Rix was interested to hear it, but appears to have made no further enquiry at the time.

Rosaline invited him to call on her in south London. It was a small house in 'very ordinary circumstances', he would later say, nothing lavish at all. He visited altogether three times, and on two occasions, Sidney was there with his mother. The subject of Swaffham Grammar School inevitably came up. Rix was thirteen years older than Sidney, but as supposed boys of the old school, they must have compared notes about masters past and present and their respective schooldays. No suspicion that he had been told a falsehood seems to have entered Rix's head, for Sidney was well able to put on the accent of a grammar school boy and perfectly capable of adding threads to the fabric that his mother had woven.

The two of them, bound in a strange oedipal marriage of convenience and deception, one nearly fifty and the other only sixteen, convinced Rix that they were the right people to look after his flat when he was away. Rosaline was working for the Red Cross. Sidney was looking for a position in the city. How more respectable could they be?

Rix invited them to move into his flat if they paid the £42 rent and said he would not charge them for use of the furniture. Rosaline agreed without hesitation. Meanwhile, Sidney found himself a job at the Army and Navy Stores in Victoria Street, a short distance from where Gerald Hamilton lived, making it very convenient for them to carry on their relationship.

It was lucky for Sidney that he was not there at midnight on Saturday 13 November, ironically the night before his brother was killed at Woolwich Arsenal. Gerald went out that weekend to a pub in the Edgware Road, which he knew well. The pickings were particularly rich. A friend introduced him to two young privates from the 1st Regiment of Life Guards, whose barracks were at Hyde Park. Harry Goy was a tall Nottinghamshire boy not yet twenty-two and had been in the Life Guards less than six months. Frank Dallas Johns was twenty and came from Guernsey. Both of them had been clerks in their civilian lives. They were a splendid sight in their uniforms, and Gerald invited them home in a cab. There was a bonus that night. An officer in the regiment was present too, in civilian dress, and came along to join the party. He was not there to keep an eye on them.

They had been indoors enough time for Gerald to have satisfied his urges and paid at least one of the young soldiers their due when his flat was raided. Far from being in bed at the time with a book, as he would later write, he was entertaining the three servicemen with post-coital whisky while wearing a skimpy yellow silk dressing gown. Inspector Tappenden of Scotland Yard, who led the raid, asked Gerald what he was doing having three soldiers in his flat, to which he replied simply, 'They are friends of mine.'

His flat was searched, and correspondence of a revealing nature, along with photographs, led to the arrests of a number of other army personnel. Johns and Goy were marched off under military guard, and Gerald was arraigned at Westminster Police Court and remanded in custody.

On 10 February 1916, he appeared at the Old Bailey charged under the Defence of the Realm Act plus gross misdemeanour and pleaded not guilty. Johns and Goy gave evidence against him, during which Johns almost fainted and had to be helped out of court. The photographs discovered were described by counsel as being of a loathsome nature but fortunately of foreign origin, which somehow excused their content. The correspondence found led to a raid on the Covent Garden Hotel, though not apparently the pubs in the Edgware Road, but for a while the moonlighting gentlemen of His Majesty's Household Cavalry had to be more circumspect in trading their wares.

Gerald was found guilty and sentenced to two years hard labour at Brixton Prison. At the end of his sentence, he would be re-arrested and interned without trial for the rest of the war under Clause 14B of the Defence of the Realm Act as a potential spy. It is doubtful he and Sidney met again, though Sidney's association with the notorious sodomite turned potential traitor would not go undiscovered. (2)

The two unlucky privates were court-martialled and discharged 'in consequence of their services being no longer required'. The fate of the officer is unknown, as is his name. Johns, boldly demonstrating that male prostitution was no barrier to joining up in wartime, enlisted a second time shortly afterwards with the 6th Battalion Oxford Bucks Light Infantry. He died in France in August 1917.

While Gerald languished in Brixton Prison, Sidney, no doubt aggrieved at the loss of his mentor but relieved that he had not been caught up in the scandal, turned seventeen and found new employment. His latest place of work was somewhere his talents would be well utilised. He found a job in a bank.

* * * * * *

Chapter Notes

1. The diary of Archibald Walker, held by Westminster Archives. Ref 1257/1

2. The colourful trajectory of the rest of Gerald Hamilton's life is best told in Tom Cullen's *The Man who was Norris*. A larger than life figure who grew larger as he consumed life, he would become known as 'the wickedest man in the world', a status elevated in no small part by himself and by his friendship with Isherwood.

CHAPTER FIVE

FLY BOYS

Cox and Company in Charing Cross was known more popularly as Cox's Bank or the Army Bank. In 1758, when Richard Cox was appointed as agent to pay the First Foot Guards, which later became the Grenadier Guards, other regiments jumped on the bandwagon, and Cox's became bankers for almost the entire armed forces. How vital this was is better appreciated when one considers how Britain's army was then scattered throughout the world, propping up the British Empire as well as fighting the Kaiser. A soldier anywhere in the world would rely on Cox's Bank to distribute his pay. On this, Cox's had a monopoly.

As a bank clerk for Cox's, Sidney would not only have to deal with money and cheque books, but he also had the opportunity to meet many of its clients, uniformed officers about to be dispatched to the front or home on leave. The sight of these young officers at Cox's dashing in and out, and the fact that every single one of them had some amorous or amusing tale to tell, was to Sidney a glamorous if somewhat untypical introduction to the world of finance. Sidney, who had now developed the same liking for uniforms as Gerald Hamilton, had a new passion. It was also to wear one.

Why he didn't join up, for he was now old enough, isn't clear. Perhaps he hated the idea of being dragged away from his precious London, a city that had got into his blood. When he was free of his desk, he would explore the West End, making new friends. Sometimes he went out with young servicemen he met at Cox's, stripping out any vowel sounds that betrayed his Norfolk origins and learning to sound more like an old Etonian. That was the background he became determined to cultivate. He was jealous of people who were called 'Sir This' and 'Sir That'. He wanted a title. If he couldn't have one legitimately, he would adopt one and hope that nobody he wished to impress would discover that he was a lowly bank clerk. For the moment, however, it would have to wait, fomenting in his mind. One thing was obvious, he couldn't be a titled gentleman until he had a cheque book.

There was a haphazard manner to the way the young officers flung their cheques about, even though a lot of them were returned RD, or Refer to Drawer. It seemed so easy to pass a cheque, even a dud one, Sidney would observe. It didn't matter, it seemed to him, if it was made out on a 'sheet of writing paper or a piece of sugar wrapping'. Neither Sidney nor his mother had ever owned such a thing. He was determined to change that and to impress her with it.

He stole one belonging to a bank customer in Hampstead, forged the customer's name, and had it made out to a grander incarnation of himself who went by the name of Sidney Herbert Granville Fox. Assuming the persona of an old Etonian, he then duly attempted to cash the cheque at another bank. His first attempt at forgery was a failure. He was found out, and the police were called in.

They went to 26 Cavendish Mansions, questioned Rosaline Fox, and searched the flat to find evidence of any other crimes her son might have committed. They were surprised by what they found. Not only had Sidney kept all his letters from Gerald Hamilton, but those from a number of senior army officers plus a young cadet. As a report by Chief Inspector Hawkins of the Metropolitan Police later summed up, 'it is quite evident from correspondence found in possession of Fox that he had been associating with Sodomites up to the time of his arrest.'

One of those 'sodomites' was Captain the Honourable Charles Stanhope Melville Bateman-Hanbury, a Justice of the Peace, of which more in a moment.

Like the Leslies before them, the bank was reluctant to prosecute, so Sidney was given a stark choice. Go to court or join the army. He didn't think twice about it. He joined the army.

His enlistment into the Army Ordnance Corps started on 2 December 1916. His first posting was to the Loyal North Lancs Regiment at Preston, but soon he was sent to the 36 Services Company Army Ordnance Corps as a storeman, in which capacity he served in various parts of the south of England. One of those places was Woolwich Arsenal, where his brother had his fatal encounter with the exploding fuse. Sidney's own rather different encounter there would benefit him greatly, as would his whole army experience.

His subsequent military career reads in part like one extended holiday in which he leapt at the chances for theft and fraud, meeting older officers and young aristocrats for nights on the town and generally having a very good time at everybody's expense but his own.

Four months into his war service, tragedy struck his family for the second time. Cecil Fox was killed in Flanders serving with the Norfolk Regiment. He was buried in the British cemetery at Duisans, near Arras. Rosaline was awarded a pension of four shillings per week. Cecil was the second of Rosaline's sons to die in consequence of the war. While continuing with her work for the Red Cross, she could now only hope that both William and Sidney would stay safe and well. Sidney had every intention of staying alive. Two brothers had perished young and would never enjoy all that life had to offer. It would be natural if he felt some guilt, but he wasn't going to let it spoil the life he had planned for himself.

Entranced by opportunities for sexual adventures and lining his pockets, Sidney had already resumed the life he had been leading while at Cox's. The teenage Don Juan was now hustling his way to being both a sexual and a social climber, a dangerous kind of companion to those who fell for his looks. The list of officers and aristocrats with whom the seventeen-year-old now consorted begins to look as though he was working his way through *Kelly's Handbook* and the *Army List*. The particular bearer of the Bateman-Hanbury name even had well-known Norfolk connections and lived only ten miles from Great Fransham at Breccles Hall, one of the finest Elizabethan houses in the country.

The Honourable Charles Stanhope Melville Bateman-Hanbury was a captain in the King's Own Royal Rifles and the Norfolk Yeomanry and a Deputy Lieutenant of the county. By the time he and Sidney met, he was attached to the military staff in London and had a town house in Mayfair to which he would invite Sidney. Breccles Hall in Addlestone, where he was Lord of the Manor, had been passed down to him by his mother, the Dowager Lady Bateman, a former rich New York widow, who on her death two years later would also leave him Shobdon Court, a handsome pile dating from the time of Charles II with magnificent views towards the Black Mountains of Wales and the Malvern Hills. If his honourable prefix, hyphenated surname, and cavalcade of middle names weren't enough to impress the boy, his family was ancient and titled. He was the fifth and youngest son of the second Baron Bateman. The Bateman and Hanbury families had been in possession of Shobdon Court for five centuries.

Forty, unmarried, and a keen sportsman, the honourable captain's position as a justice might make it seem unlikely he would take the risk of being among those who would write letters to Sidney's home. On the stock exchange, however, he was an inveterate and reckless gambler. Prior to their meeting, he incurred speculative losses over a period of ten years amounting to £138,000. He formed and dissolved companies, dealt in landed properties and works of art with no great flair for financial genius, and bred racehorses. Heavy rates of interest and law costs would eat away at the rest, and he eventually became insolvent. It was nothing unusual and almost expected of the aristocracy who had fortunes to play with, so perhaps a dalliance with a boy of seventeen for a man in his position was just another game of chance.

An aversion to risk, however, was not one of the qualities possessed by the next addition to Sidney's growing circle of older admirers.

He said in his life story that it was at Woolwich Arsenal he met an army colonel who worked as commandant for an auxiliary hospital in the north, and that on weekends off he would take the train to Crewe and be treated royally by his new friend. Sidney refrained from mentioning his name, but 'Colonel X' came to London and introduced him to all manner of titled friends. Sidney, by dint of that new friendship and the money lavished on him, began a round of meeting beautiful actresses, entertaining stage stars and going to wild parties, all while employed as a storeman for the Army Ordnance Corps, probably not the punishment that Cox's Bank and the police had in mind.

Colonel X was Colonel Percy Holland CB, ex Indian Army, who had been called out of retirement to head a brigade in France. Aged fifty-five, he was a veteran of numerous campaigns in Egypt, the North-West Frontier and China, and had for seven years before his retirement commanded the 47th Sikhs. He had been married for twenty-three years and awarded his CB only three years before meeting Sidney. With his handsome curling moustache and a distinguished military career behind him, Percy Holland was everybody's conception of a straight-up, Eton-educated British army officer. Given his predilection for men, young men in particular, it is hardly surprising that he developed a deep liking for Sidney. Holland's interest in the theatre—he had appeared in amateur productions and Red Cross entertainments himself—chimed with Sidney's love of the West End.

Sidney had found two new benefactors. That number would soon rise to three.

Exactly how he managed to pass himself off as the Honourable Sidney Harry Fox while working as an army storekeeper is one of the minor mysteries of his career, but it is evidenced by the fact that Holland addressed future mail to him as such. Perhaps when one considers that he was able to pose as an old boy of Swaffham Grammar School to another, it is not so surprising. Many titled people took menial jobs to help the war effort, and Sidney was well capable of peppering his genealogy with gentlemen rather than agricultural workers and railway servants. Holland's eyes must have been pretty well clouded with stars, and not just the theatrical kind. Totally smitten by his new young friend, he treated him generously wherever they went, both up north and in London, where there were theatres and restaurants galore.

It has been implied that Sidney was blackmailing the middle-aged officer and that the warm and fatherly affection he described was merely a front, but blackmail could take many forms, from out and out menaces to the mere knowledge that if one didn't play the game and continue to provide the funds, the consequences could be disastrous. On the other hand, Sidney had never enjoyed the love of a real father. Holland was more than happy to play along with that role.

Colonel Holland introduced him to another aristocrat, by reputation a man whose idea of heaven was going to the theatre every night of his life. Whether meeting Sidney Fox was the young Lord Lathom's idea of heaven is impossible to know, but for Sidney, he was the only one he would give a name to and whose friendship he would boast about in his life story without recourse to any pseudonym, calling him 'one of the finest and kindest of men'.

Edward William Bootle-Wilbraham, 3rd Earl of Lathom and, as it happened, the last of his line, was known as Ned. Only four years older than Sidney, he had attained his majority while in the trenches. As a boy of fifteen, he inherited large estates in Lancashire with valuable mineral deposits and would become, for a time, one of the wealthiest members of the House of Lords. Sidney was drawn to the young Lathom like a wasp to a pot of jam.

The sweetness didn't end there. Lathom lived a hedonistic lifestyle and spent his money on his friends, a recipe that brought many hangers-on, like Sidney, into his circle. He had developed a talent for the stage and built a theatre on his estate for his workers. He financed productions in which he was interested and gave money to hard-up actors whom he scarcely knew. In time he would become a playwright, though not a successful one. His first play *Wet Paint* would be banned by the censor for being too sexually explicit and demolished by the critics on its American opening. It featured two male friends in a bachelor apartment in Mayfair, one of whom lived way beyond his means and wanted desperately to live more like the people he read about in the *Tatler*.

The character sounds suspiciously like Sidney. Lathom may even have based it on him.

The most astonishing step in Sidney's military career then took place. It was Colonel Holland, he said, who helped him get into the Royal Flying Corps as a cadet. This is a story which, for years to come, Sidney related to anyone who would listen, with an increasing number of embellishments. While it sounds like fantasy, the story does contain a grain of truth. The glamour of the RFC, with its motto of *Per ardua ad astra* (Through adversity to the stars), in the early days of the war, cannot be over-estimated. It was then the reserve of the elite, young men from upper-class families who styled themselves Knights of the Air. If one had the right background or professed to have the same, enough bluster to carry it off, plus the sponsorship of a senior army officer who would vouch, however mistakenly, for your credentials, it was relatively easy to walk into. The RFC in its early days was as much a club for young gentlemen as a service. Their new recruit was suddenly swapping the duties of a storeman for the far more exciting and exhilarating prospect of training to be a pilot or observer in one of the thirty-four aircraft at their command in the 2nd Squadron of the RFC at Farnborough.

Being admitted to the Royal Flying Corps, however, was a far cry from actually serving abroad or flying a plane. Sidney never left the ground. For most of his time he was ill with tonsillitis, and his training was curtailed while he went into the Queen Alexandra Military Hospital in London. He had his adenoids removed, and they also discovered a long-standing condition in his right ear which caused deafness, not a good attribute for a pilot. He was rejected by the RFC, almost as quickly as he had been admitted, on medical grounds. The Red Baron had nothing to fear.

The documentation for the Royal Flying Corps records the address to which he intended going on his leaving hospital. He might have been expected to put down Rosaline's address at Cavendish Mansions, but he didn't. Her son had other ideas of what convalescing meant. Instead, Sidney was invited to stay and recuperate at 62 Curzon Street in Mayfair, the London address of Captain the Honourable Charles Stanhope Melville Bateman-Hanbury, Lord of the Manor of Breccles Hall and Norfolk Justice of the Peace.

Sidney was having a very good war indeed. Captain Bateman-Hanbury would survive his friendship with Sidney. So would Lord Lathom.

Colonel Holland did not.

* * * * * *

CHAPTER SIX

THE HONOURABLE
SIDNEY HARRY FOX

While Sidney was languishing in hospital, he kept himself occupied by distributing mail to the other patients. The envelope containing one item of mail was slightly torn, and Sidney could see that it was a cheque book addressed to an officer on the ward, Lieutenant Ingle. His fascination for cheque books and their potential was not diminished. The sight of those strips of paper on which one only needed to write a figure and sign one's name was too tempting. He purloined it. Now he had a cheque book in his pocket, his passport to money of his own.

One day he took the train to Brighton, where he called on a Mrs Hoffman, a friend of Sir John and Constance Leslie. Sir John had died shortly after Sidney's leaving Manchester Square, but the immediate family, including Lady Constance, her son and Lady Theodosia Bagot, still took an interest in him, hoping he had mended his ways. They must have been relieved that he had joined the army, believing that it would make a man of him, preferably an honest one. If so, their hopes were wide of the mark. The Leslies' pet Cupid still had a quiver full of arrows, but they were all aimed at his own advancement.

When Sidney presented himself at the elderly Mrs Hoffman's in Salisbury Road, Hove, he did so not as their errant ex-page but as one of the Leslies' many grandchildren. He had perfected the patter of the class and knew the Leslie family well enough to be able to pass himself off as one of them to the unsuspecting lady. Then the real purpose of his visit emerged. He wanted to cash a cheque.

Had Sidney attempted to cash one of Lieutenant Ingle's cheques in London, he might have got away with it, but instead he left a trail that would be his undoing. Mrs Hoffman was unable to cash the cheque, but she referred him to her greengrocer, Mr Arthur Breach, in Western Road. Breach obligingly cashed the cheque, which was for the sum of five pounds, a considerable sum in 1917, after which Sidney returned to London. It was a convoluted exercise, but Sidney enjoyed playing the role as much as receiving the money.

An Assistant Provost Marshall at the War Office, with responsibility for the Eastern Division and the unlikely name of William Glynes Bruty, happened to be on holiday in Brighton. He was a solicitor by profession and had become attached to the War Office on the outbreak of hostilities. Captain Bruty got to hear of the young man who had passed a dud cheque at the greengrocer's shop in Western Road and which had been returned RD. It is astonishing that with thousands dying in the trenches in Europe and the threat of zeppelins coming across the channel, not to mention

German spies, he should have bothered himself with a five-pound cheque passed by an unknown youth in a greengrocer's. But bother himself he did, probably because of his civilian occupation as a solicitor rather than as a soldier. Wheels, now completely out of Sidney's power to derail, were set in motion.

Bruty obtained a description of Sidney from Mrs Hoffman and an account of his visit and realised he was no relative of the Leslies but was instead the page boy with whose services they had dispensed the previous year. He then sent a military policeman in plain clothes to call on Rosaline Fox in Hampstead. Startlingly, she volunteered the information that her son, whom she now referred to as Lieutenant Fox, was a member of the Royal Automobile Club in Pall Mall. If Rosaline really believed this nonsense, she had been duped on a scale that almost defies belief.

In the early days of motoring, the Royal Automobile Club was a hallowed institution. They had effectively started the sport of road racing, one event being the 1903 Gordon Bennett race outside Dublin. Membership fees were high, twenty-five guineas to join and ten guineas annually. Since the beginning of the war, the club house was put at the disposal of the armed services. Pall Mall had become an officers' club, with part of the building used by the Red Cross. It was, therefore, nothing unusual that a letter should be waiting for Sidney addressed to the Honourable S.H. Fox to await collection, as others like it had been hand-delivered before. The person who was leaving the letters was an elderly officer with an Eton accent and a handsome curled moustache.

Captain Bruty accompanied the plain-clothes military policeman to the RAC, where they opened the current letter. It was of an amorous and compromising nature.

They sealed it again and awaited Fox's arrival. Sidney arrived that evening, at 7.30pm, wearing the uniform of a Second Lieutenant in the RFC, which he had left a few weeks earlier. Where and how he got it was never explained, but such an acquisition was not beyond Sidney. He opened the letter, read it, and, unsuspecting, threw the pieces into a wastepaper basket. He had obviously learned not to store letters, but his instincts were not so well honed as they should have been.

As the pieces were retrieved by his colleague, Captain Bruty stepped forward and came face to face with the young man he had been chasing since his holiday in Brighton.

One of the first questions he asked was, 'Are you entitled to the courtesy title of Honourable?' (1)

Sidney replied that he was and told the captain that his mother's father was a gentleman.

'Doubtless,' said Captain Bruty, 'but that does not entitle you to the prefix.'

'I thought it did,' said Sidney.

'Are you a member of this club?' he asked.

'Certainly I am,' Sidney answered brazenly.

'When did you join?'

Less confidently, Sidney explained, 'Well, I filled up the papers for joining.'

'That does not make you a member.' Bruty switched abruptly to the subject of the uniform. 'Are you an officer?'

Sidney tried to sound just as confident, but it was clear he was coming unstuck.

'Certainly I am.'

'When did you get your commission?'

'I got a chit to say I was going to be gazetted when I was in the hospital,' Sidney floundered, knowing the game was up.

'That does not make you an officer, and you are not an officer. You must come with me.'

At police headquarters, Sidney was made to turn out his pockets, and the first thing they found was the cheque book he had used in Brighton. His private life was exposed further when they discovered some rouge and a booklet of scented writing paper. Similar kinds of items had been found in Gerald Hamilton's flat. If there was one thing Sidney was clearly not, it was an officer and a gentleman.

The torn-up letter was pieced together and pasted on a sheet of tissue paper. It was signed only with the initials PH, but on the notepaper of another club of which his correspondent was a member. Sidney then admitted that the writer was Colonel Percy Holland.

Sidney appeared at Hove Magistrates Court on 21 December, where his barrister Mr Trangmar asked the bench to deal lightly with him as he was the son of respectable parents, had a good situation as a valet, and that three of his brothers had been killed in the war, a statement which contained three blatant untruths.

The magistrates retired and, on their return, said the offence had been a deliberately planned scheme. They sentenced Sidney to three months hard labour in Portsmouth Prison. As they were no doubt determined to get at least some active service out of him, the sentence was to include further training for the army.

Percy Holland's punishment was cruel, for an officer with an unblemished war record, though it could have had worse consequences. He was cashiered and removed from the army, being 'unworthy any longer to remain a member'. He was stripped of his rank and CB.

His case had a curious sequel.

Colonel Holland had earlier been president of a court considering evidence of indecent conduct against another decorated war soldier, Colonel Hugh de Berdt Hovell of the Worcestershire Regiment, known as Mad Jack, one of whose accusers had committed suicide. Holland judged that though Colonel Hovell was 'undoubtedly eccentric in his manner and methods of dealing with his men'—a euphemistic phrase if ever there was one—there was no ground for specific charges. Hovell was nevertheless removed from his command because of the strong wording. After the war, he unsuccessfully tried to sue Percy Holland, who was by then no longer a colonel, for libelling him in his report and ruining his career. The irony of one disgraced officer suing another was not lost on anyone.

Meanwhile, Sidney served out his sentence and went back under military escort to join an infantry battalion, the 3rd Reserve Battalion Wiltshire Regiment. In less than a month, he was back on the sick list. This time there would be no visits to the bright lights of London.

* * * * * *

Chapter Note

1. The conversation was reported in Frynn Tennyson Jesse's introduction to *The Trial of Sidney Fox* (1934) in the *Notable British Trials* series, Hodge and Co. Jesse enjoyed the opportunity to meet many people associated with the Fox case, including Captain Bruty and James Cassels, Fox's barrister. I have used the exact words used by Miss Jesse and attributed to Captain Bruty.

CHAPTER SEVEN

AN INGENIOUS TEENAGE FORGER

Rosaline was determined to enjoy life as much as she could in Sidney's absence. Working for the Red Cross was satisfying, but if her son could be kept in funds by doting elderly colonels and homosexual spies, she was entitled to have a bit of fun of her own. Around this time she met up with Jim Nelson, the thatcher's son from Necton, who in her childhood had been the boy who lived down the lane from her married cousins. Nelson had been living in north London most of his life and was employed as a motor-bus driver with the London General Omnibus Company. Originally, the buses had been pulled by horses, but horse-drawn omnibuses gradually disappeared aa the new century progressed, and by 1910 there were scarcely any left on the roads. Bus driving was one of the highest paid working-class jobs to be had in the capital, and Nelson took home five pounds a week.

He was married, but his wife had left him. Drivers frequently bemoaned the fact that their job gave them little time for family life or any other kind of life for that matter. He didn't know where his wife was or indeed if she was still alive, and it appears that he had no children. Rosaline was fifty-two, still attractive, and a fair match, for they shared not only memories of growing up in the Norfolk countryside but many friends as well. Nelson lived on his own not far away, in Fairbridge Road, Hornsey, and it might well have been his presence that made Rosaline want to move to the Hampstead district in the first place. By the time Sidney came out of the army, his mother had taken herself a lover, and Jim Nelson had become a regular visitor to 26 Cavendish Mansions, very often staying the night.

Sidney spent most of his remaining army service in hospital, suffering from what he claimed was epilepsy. He said it was wearing a gas mask during training that made him collapse and brought it on, something he had previously grown out of at the age of seven. Whether this was true or not, he was moved around from one medical institution to another until his discharge on 13 February 1919, well after the war had ended. He was medically examined, and the epilepsy was detailed in his records as constitutional, meaning it had nothing to do with the wearing of gas masks or any other part of his training. He left the army with a pension of eight shillings a week.

Rosaline wrote to him in prison and in hospital, telling him that whatever happened he would always have a place with her. Cavendish Mansions was still his home and would always be for as long as she lived there. She continued to work as a nurse for the Red Cross and, through that organisation, met Walpurga, Lady Paget. Born with the less easily remembered name of Countess

Walpurga Ehrengarde Helena von Hothenhal, she had married Sir Augustus Berkeley Paget, the British Ambassador in Copenhagen. She was eighty years old, a strict vegetarian, and had once been a lady-in-waiting to the young Princess Victoria. She was very much the kind of acquaintance that Rosaline liked to cultivate, and they became great friends, or so Sidney would maintain.

Mrs Annie Tanthony, the wife of the caretaker who lived in flat 25, noticed a short, thickset and round-shouldered man who was apparently sleeping at the Foxes' as he was frequently seen leaving in the morning. She also observed that Sidney was often there when the man stayed, a perfect example of how morals had declined at Cavendish Mansions. Her husband challenged the gentleman one morning over his habit of slinking in the back way and asked why he didn't use the proper main entrance, for these early morning departures were clearly suggestive of a lover. It may also, of course, have meant that the gentleman had to get up to drive a bus. The Tanthonys described him as about forty-five. Jim Nelson was sixty-three. Either Nelson was a very well-preserved man in his sixties, or Rosaline had another lover, which was not outside the bounds of possibility. It was also not unlikely that Sidney had taken to bringing a gentleman friend home. Whatever the domestic arrangement, it was clear that Cavendish Mansions was not a place where they could enjoy much privacy. To have proprietors living next door, audacious enough to challenge their guests, was not an ideal situation, but Rosaline was determined to stay there as long as possible.

This she made clear when Henry Rix came home and wanted his flat back. Rix had transferred to the Royal

Navy Air Service during the war but was now in the reserve, which meant that prior to his eventual discharge he was able to return for periods. An unpleasant surprise awaited him. Rosaline and Sidney had been occupying the flat now for the best part of five years, and Rosaline refused to move.

Rix was furious, but legally he could do nothing as it was a furnished flat, and he had sublet the property without any restrictions or time limit. He set about removing all of his furniture plus the curtains and moved elsewhere so that mother and son had to furnish it again themselves. But at least they were still in Hampstead, which pleased Rosaline.

Sidney needed another job and, amazingly, as he now had a criminal record, found it with another bank at twenty-nine shillings a week. Whether Grindlay's of Parliament Square were aware of his record isn't known. They were an old established house which had been around for ninety years. Their once grand offices today still bear the name Grindlay's Bank forged into the metal railings. They had started up by arranging passage to and from India for customers and their baggage. Over the years, they added banking activities to their services and were principally bankers to the Indian Army with offices in Simla, Delhi, Calcutta and Bombay. It was an opportunity for Sidney to turn a corner in his life and perhaps be sent abroad to one of the bank's Indian branches, which Sidney said was offered him soon after joining.

True to form, it was another kind of corner he turned. He claimed in his life story that he was genuinely attempting to go straight but met an old acquaintance from the days when he swanned around London in an officer's uniform. His friend smacked him heartily on the back, enquired after him, invited him to dinner, and after copious amounts of wine, they drifted on to a night club where they met and befriended two 'beautiful and jolly chorus girls'. The chorus girls may well have existed, but what is known is that he met and became close friends with a Jewish leather worker from the East End called Alfred Lupson, who made suitcases and travelling bags.

Lupson, who was fifteen years his senior, said they met in Hampstead, so if not the Heath, it may have been the King William, which had a reputation as a meeting place for homosexual men even then. He lived in a flat in Powis Square, Bayswater, and after an initial invitation back to his flat, perhaps not simply to look at examples of Lupson's skilled workmanship, Sidney began a friendship that would last almost until his death. The impression one gets of Lupson is that he could be opened like a book. This was in stark contrast to the charming, deceptive Sidney, whose pages were so stuck together—like his charity collecting exercise— that you couldn't read him at all. Lupson claimed that he was never terribly sure what Sidney did for a living, that he thought he had something to do with insurance.

They would quickly become boon companions, exploring the West End of London together, going to the theatre, drinking and going to saunas which were popular places for men to have sex. Sidney was becoming known around town as 'the kid'. Lupson met Rosaline Fox on several occasions. She was by now no stranger to her son's predilections. In 1919, even though London was a city casting off wartime restrictions and enjoying its reputation as a free-wheeling pleasure-seeking capital with fewer social barriers, no ordinary mother would normally turn a blind eye to a homosexual son keeping company with men of his own kind, as well as living off older ones.

But then Rosaline and Sidney were no normal or ordinary mother and son. At least a woman wouldn't come along and take Sidney away from her. No man either, she thought, for it was rare in those days for two men to form binding, lasting relationships and move in together. If she could just keep him out of prison, it would satisfy her. She was getting no younger, and a son in prison could not care for her. Sidney was her insurance policy.

At the same time, Sidney remained friends with Lord Lathom, who continued to invite him on rounds of stage doors, wild parties and night clubs, and to the theatre where Lathom was almost invariably seen on first nights. Soho was like a magnet. Every evening after work, Sidney would hurry home to get into evening dress for a good night out. His wealthy friends introduced him to tailors from whom he could obtain credit. It was only a matter of time before he turned once more to fraud to finance his lifestyle.

And this time, it was so elaborate and necessitated so many train journeys to different parts of the country, that one has to question if Sidney's entire aim was just to line his pocket. There was a recklessness, a passion, about his criminal activities that bore comparison to his old friend and mentor Gerald Hamilton, who had been released from internment after the war and gone back to Rome. Even the police would admit that the series of frauds Sidney committed at Grindlay's demonstrated remarkable ingenuity for a teenager. So ingenious were they that several other employees were initially suspected, while the young man who had recently joined them had been earmarked for early promotion. It would not be surprising if Sidney assisted one or two of his colleagues into the frame as he had done on previous occasions.

On 23 July, a communication was received from Mr Owen Jones, who had been a customer of the bank for seven years. He was staying at the Bedford Hotel in Brighton and desired thirty pounds to be sent to him there. In the days before high-street banks became common in town centres, it was not unusual for servicemen to contact Grindlay's and ask for money to be delivered. Representatives of Grindlay's would meet troop ships returning from abroad with sums of money to help their customers get settled.

Mr Jones' money was sent by registered package the same day, but by the time it got there, he had cancelled his reservation. However, he turned up the following day, signed for the package and left. He never returned to the Bedford Hotel. On 5 August, Mr Jones was at the Imperial Hotel, Russell Square in London, from where he wrote asking for a small book of twelve cheques to be sent to him there.

Three days later, Mr Jones, described as age 24 to 25, with a fair complexion and fair hair, clean-shaven, dressed in a grey lounge suit and grey trilby hat, well-educated and of gentlemanly appearance, called at the Civil Service Co-operative Society Stores in the Haymarket where he opened an account with a cheque for one hundred pounds, giving his address as Welbeck House, New Steine Brighton, and Chalcot Gardens in Hampstead. He then proceeded to buy a number of items, including two pairs of curtains, a number of curtain rings, and two wooden flower stands, the kinds of items that would go some small way to refurnishing a flat lived in by a mother and son who had fallen on hard times.

Further purchases followed until Mr Jones said he was leaving town and took sixty-seven pounds out of his account in cash, leaving a small amount to keep the account open. He also left a specimen signature for the future, as was the practice of the store. This happened to be an excellent imitation of the signature of the real Mr Owen Jones, who at that time was living in Diss, Norfolk, and planning to emigrate to Australia. He had been, remarkably, a genuine cadet in the Royal Flying Corps.

Around the same time, a bank customer called Lieutenant Ingle (it beggars belief that he may have been the same Lieutenant Ingle whose cheque book Fox stole while he was in hospital with tonsillitis) wrote to the bank asking for seventy-five pounds to be sent to him at the Adelphi Hotel in Liverpool. Then a Mr C.W. Hope requested that fifty pounds be sent to him at the Metropole in Brighton, from where the money was collected by a young bank clerk when he finished work for the day. Sidney was clearly on a roll. As W.H.P. Gorringe, yet another bank customer, he asked for twenty-five pounds to be delivered to him at the Red Lion Hotel in Cambridge. Sidney had a holiday due (from the bank but clearly not from his criminal activities), and as he was going to Edinburgh, he wrote to the Red Lion asking for the money to be forwarded to the Royal Hotel there. He didn't get to Edinburgh and never saw the money. He came home to his mother's house prior to his intended Scottish trip and found the police waiting. He was carrying a suitcase and had on him a silver cigarette case which, as Owen Jones, he had also purchased from the Co-operative Stores.

His frauds came to light when the real Mr Owen Jones asked the bank to send three hundred pounds to his credit at the Commonwealth Bank, Melbourne, in preparation for his move to Australia. He was sent a statement and immediately contacted Grindlay's saying he had never stayed at the Metropole in Brighton or the Imperial in London, nor had he ever received such sums in money.

Sidney was charged at Cannon Row Police Station and the next day remanded in custody at Bow Street Police Court. At the Old Bailey, he pleaded guilty—he could scarcely do anything else—and was sent to Wormwood Scrubs for eight months. He wrote a letter to the judge saying that twenty-nine shillings a week wasn't sufficient to pay for his lunches, his train fare, to support his widowed mother and to dress suitably for a job in a bank. He didn't mention also having to pay back a moneylender in Conduit Street. Not surprisingly, His Lordship was unsympathetic.

Rosaline not only suffered the shock of having her favourite son sent away until the spring of the following year but the ignominy of having their new furnishings confiscated and returned to the Co-operative Stores. Nevertheless, she wrote to Sidney once more, telling him he would always have a roof over his head with her, as she would do many times.

* * * * * *

CHAPTER EIGHT

RAFFLES, AND THE SECRET LIFE OF MARGARET CHADWICK ABELL

On 19 May 1920, Sidney was released from Wormwood Scrubs. He had spent his twenty-first birthday inside, so to celebrate his coming-of-age, he treated himself to a couple of belated presents from Harrods department store. Adopting the pseudonym of Stanley Fox, he chose a diamond ring worth forty guineas and a gold cigarette case priced at forty-four pounds, and directed that they should be sent to his father's address at New Malden in Essex. The occupant was a well-known Harrods account customer whom Sidney claimed that he knew. The jewellery was despatched, while Sidney complained of the delay and threatened to cancel the order. Part of his *modus operandi* was to make trouble. People in stores were less likely to suspect you of wrongdoing if you made a fuss.

His next audacious move was to call at the house in New Malden, produce the Harrods counterfoils, and say that a mistake had been made because of a similarity of names. He took possession of the packet, went back to Harrods, and tried to exchange the ring for one worth a hundred pounds. While there, he took the opportunity to order the most expensive clothing he could, saying that he was going on a continental journey and that his manservant would receive it at a railway station cloakroom.

The only journey Sidney embarked on was back to prison, this time Wandsworth, for eight months. From his cell, he wrote to the Home Office, his letter full of the usual inexactitudes, as well as poor grammar and punctuation. He might have posed as an Eton scholar, but he did not write like one.

'I do not think that the magistrate who sentenced me fully understood my case,' he told them. 'Why I committed this crime was I could not get employment when I left school to join the army I was working up for a profession, having served in France and elsewhere I naturally could not keep up my studies, with the result, when I came home I was not fitted for anything and could not get work, God knows I tried hard enough. That my mother is at the moment very seriously ill, my father being dead, and my three brothers who were killed in the war, I am the only one left to support her. I plead sir that you will consider my appeal for her sake. Sir John Leslie, Bart, who came to the police court to speak for me, is finding me employment on my being discharged from prison.'

He had never served in France, and it is doubtful Rosaline was really ill, though it is true the Leslie family were genuinely concerned.

Sir John Leslie of Manchester Square had died four years earlier. The Sir John who came to the police court was his only son and heir, Colonel John Leslie, who was married to a sister of Lady Randolph Churchill. It says something that Sidney managed to hold on to the support of a family as aristocratic as the Leslies. He had robbed them, impersonated a member of their family, and yet they still felt their cherubic former page boy turned charming confidence trickster was capable of being reformed. At the time of his previous conviction, Colonel Leslie had asked that Sidney be sent to borstal instead of prison, but the medical officer at Wormwood Scrubs believed Sidney was a genuine epileptic and as such was unsuitable for borstal training. He was prepared to consider that Sidney might be a mental defective but couldn't or wouldn't certify him as such.

Sidney's brother William would have had no such compunction, and this became a fierce bone of contention between him and Rosaline. As time went by, regardless of the fact William's young wife used to visit her in London with Rosaline's granddaughter, she spoke less and less of her eldest son. Like Sidney, she would start to adopt the fiction that she had three sons who had been killed in the war, not two. William would become a non-person, written out of her life. Anyone who attacked or did not support her beloved Sidney was no friend, or son, of hers.

When Sidney was released from Wandsworth in 1921, once again he went back to his mother who, he said, begged him to turn over a new leaf. He promised her that he would and once more set out on the 'dreary task of looking for employment'. He found a job obtaining orders for advertisements, but it was not the exciting life he craved. Two months later he was in trouble again.

This time it wasn't a bank or a department store he would be caught defrauding. It was a young woman. And this time he had an accomplice which, for Sidney Harry Fox, the lone operator, was a rarity.

Walter Tarrant was four years older than Sidney and worked as a clerk for the Inland Revenue in Croydon. He was short in stature, slightly effeminate, wore pince-nez spectacles and walked with a limp, the consequence it was said of a deformed foot. More likely it was the result of a war injury, for he had been wounded in Salonica before being demobilised two years earlier. Tarrant came from a family of war heroes. Four brothers had all been wounded on the Western Front and in the Dardanelles, one had been a prisoner of war in Germany, and another, Corporal Harry Tarrant, had died in France in October 1918. Their parents had been sent a letter from the King, commending them on their sacrifices. Like Sidney, Walter had joined the Wiltshires, though his own war experiences were very different, including twice being court-martialled, once in France and once in Egypt. Before war broke out, he had brought more shame than honour to his parents by being bound over for importuning men for immoral purposes.

Tarrant claimed that he first met Sidney in Croydon. Sidney told him he was the son of a millionaire, which Tarrant apparently believed. Tarrant told Sidney his father was a well-known public figure in Croydon, whereas he had been a railway plate layer. From the start, they were made for each other.

Shortly afterwards, Tarrant left his employment, stealing fourteen pounds he had helped raise for a staff dance. He and Sidney took a flat together in Chelsea, the only occasion in which it is known that Sidney ever voluntarily moved away from Rosaline, except for his brief stay with Captain Bateman-Hanbury in Curzon Street. Whether or not Sidney and Walter remained just friends or became lovers, which was quite possible, they were soon conspirators in a much greater enterprise. The young man from the good heroic family in Croydon introduced the millionaire's son to a new venture, hotel theft. As it did for Sidney, expensive jewellery had an attraction for Tarrant. And what better places to find it than in expensive hotels, where rich young women came down to dinner in the evening adorned with fine rings, glittering necklaces, and bracelets encrusted with sparkling diamonds.

There is no doubt Tarrant had been at the game before he met Sidney, who now became a willing pupil. They travelled the country, staying in places as far apart as Manchester, Bognor, Folkestone, Buxton and Torquay, always residing in fashionable hotels and not, of course, paying their bills. Tarrant used the alias Reginald Wynne, a name that suggested more upper-class credentials. But throughout that summer, when the spate of meticulously planned hotel thefts came to the attention of the press, they would give the as yet unknown perpetrator another name, Raffles, after the fictional gentleman jewel thief created by E.W. Hornung, the brother of Sir Arthur Conan Doyle.

It was an accolade that no doubt delighted the plate-layer's son from Croydon. Raffles was the antithesis of Sherlock Holmes, who with his very own Watson, an old schoolfriend called Bunny Manders, committed daring robberies, always clothed impeccably in evening dress. The stories were popular, though Holmes' creator felt it was wrong to make fictional heroes out of criminals.

Sidney was no Bunny Manders and could not hope to achieve heights like that. He would be referred to in the press, who had no idea of his name, merely as the accomplice who aided this young grand master of crime.

At the Embassy Hotel in Bayswater, Tarrant noted that a Miss Isobel Macrae came down to breakfast without the rings she had been wearing the night before. Tarrant gained entry to her room and found them secreted under her pillow. Within half an hour, he had sold them at London's Hatton Garden, probably before she had finished breakfast. At the Cadogan Hotel, he kept careful watch on his victim for some time. He entered the room of a Miss Helen Davis by means of a master key kept in the lift for the benefit of residents, a nice gesture also to prospective hotel thieves. On that occasion, he made off with £3,500 worth of jewels.

They would fall out after the job in Bognor when Sidney, according to his criminal associate, had decamped from their flat in Chelsea, leaving him penniless. There was no honour between thieves. But the robbery which was to be the downfall of both of them was not at a hotel but at an apartment in Kensington.

On 20 May 1921, Miss Marguerite Odell of 6 Rugby Mansions in Bishop Kings Road, West Kensington, received a phone call from a friend asking to meet her at the Savoy Hotel. She promptly left the flat in the charge of her maid and was observed by two men, one of whom was heard by the janitor saying to the other, 'She's not wearing her furs.'

The two men immediately appeared at the door and told the maid, Annie Savill, that they had an appointment with her mistress. The maid informed them that she was out, but they were persistent and said they would wait for her. They asked if they could have tea, and the maid brought it to them. While one was drinking it and talking to distract her, the other went to phone the hotel but was seen going into Miss Odell's bedroom. The man, who answered Sidney's description, told the maid he had made a mistake and was looking for the lavatory, and then later that he had got through to the hotel and that they were going to meet her there. Meanwhile, arriving at the hotel to find no friend waiting for her, Miss Odell, realising it was a bogus call, tried to phone home, but the wires had been cut. Before she could return, the pair had made off with a set of sable furs, a coney seal coat, plus cutlery and jewellery to the value of £1,200. The furs were later pawned in Liverpool.

There was clearly much more to this story than the bald facts reported in the newspapers. Rugby Mansions was one of the most expensive addresses in the area. Miss Odell was thirty-one. For a young single woman at that time to be in sole possession of such valuable luxuries and with a maid to care for her domestic needs suggests that she had an income greater than one would expect of a private secretary. Indeed, that was how she described herself on one of the numerous cabin class voyages she took across the Atlantic. Just for good measure, Marguerite Odell wasn't even her real name. Even a victim of crime was entitled to have an alias, and the high-living Miss Odell had a good reason for hers.

A few weeks later, Sidney was arrested and charged at the West London Police Court with committing the crime, along with another man 'not in custody'. How the police caught him was not mentioned. Neither was the name of the other man. Sidney was described in the *Illustrated Police News* as smartly dressed and clean-shaven and of no fixed address. Perhaps, in this case, he didn't want his mother to know he was in trouble again. He was sent to Brixton, which was then a remand prison.

When the 1921 census was taken on 19 June that year, the enumerator found him there awaiting trial and recorded him as Sidney Harry Fox, aged twenty-one, born Norfolk, described as a student of engineering at the Royal College in Edinburgh. Sidney's habit of lying for no good purpose never failed him, even under dire circumstances. On this occasion he failed himself. The Royal College in Edinburgh was of surgeons, not engineering. No matter; he would soon be free. The police had bigger fish to catch and fry.

Two days later, he appeared at the Central Criminal Court before Sir Robert Wallace KC. The Central Criminal Court wasn't just the famous Old Bailey building but was held at numerous session houses north and south of the river. There, he was charged with stealing one coat and other articles and receiving same, valued together at £1,200, from 6 Rugby Mansions. It appears that no evidence was put forward. He was found not guilty and discharged. Given his quick arrest, and the fact the maid was able to identify him, he was lucky to escape going to prison, the only time in his life he would ever do it. There can be no doubt that Sidney escaped prosecution and had the charge against him dropped because he helped the police track down his one-time friend and accomplice and was prepared to give evidence against him. If nothing else, Sidney was true to form.

In October, Divisional Detective Inspector Burton, accompanied by two sergeants, tracked down Walter Tarrant to the silver ring at Alexandra Park Racecourse, where he was watching the end of a race through his tortoiseshell-rimmed pince-nez spectacles. These glasses were a feature of his description, one that had been circulated widely, but in spite of the fact that he was never without them, he had so far eluded the best brains of Scotland Yard. Now they had finally 'checked the career of one of the most notorious hotel thieves in England'. His latest crime had been the theft at the Cadogan Hotel in Chelsea. He had on him when arrested a pearl scarf-pin, a diamond ring, and other jewellery from that robbery, along with sixty pounds in the lining of his waistcoat.

'Yes, I am Reginald Wynne, the man you want,' he said, using his alias but hardly able to deny his guilt. 'I am glad it is over because I intended to go straight after the Cadogan Hotel job.'

There was little evidence he had intended to go straight. After escaping from that job, he had taken a taxicab with his haul to Mount Street in Mayfair, the address of some of the most prestigious hotels in London, just to put the police off the scent. He then spent the night at the Imperial Hotel in Russell Square, where he left the key from the Cadogan job.

The newspapers made much of the real-life Raffles, who had hired expensive cars to drive between jobs and made love to pretty young women, a rather more inaccurate and romantic image than the one he merited. He confessed to all the hotel thefts, along with the robbery at Rugby Mansions. On being sentenced to four years at Parkhurst prison on the Isle of Wight, the gentleman thief broke down in tears and had to be helped from the dock.

Because Tarrant made a full confession, Sidney, in the end, did not have to go to court.

It was not an episode of which Sidney could have been very proud. The absence of honour between thieves extended to friends and possibly lovers as well in this case. He left Walter Tarrant out of his life story completely, along with much that did not do him credit. On his release from Parkhurst, Tarrant obtained forged references and found himself a job as a servant to an Edith Matts, a 'London dressmaker' of 148 Brompton Road from whom he stole a quantity of jewellery. Described in a number of newspaper reports as 'effeminate looking' and as a 'male house parlourmaid', an image which sits at total variance from that of Raffles, he was sent to prison for a further fifteen months. He ended his days at the family home in Croydon, working as a builder's clerk and living with an unmarried sister. He died aged 80 and left £10,000 in his will. (1)

The real mystery revolved around the victim of the Rugby Mansions robbery. When Tarrant's trial was reported, Miss Marguerite Odell became Mrs Margaret Abell. No explanation was offered. It may have been that the original reports got her name wrong, but Margaret Abell wasn't her real name either.

Neither was she Margaret Chadwick Abell as she appeared in the electoral register for 6 Rugby Mansions. There was no such person.

A little research into the crime proves the adage that everyone has something to hide. Sidney may not have wanted his mother to discover that he was a budding professional hotel thief rather than a common crook and forger, nor his new friend and accomplice to know that he wasn't really a millionaire's son but the offspring of a railwayman. Walter Tarrant adhered to his alias of Reginald Wynne, which was the name in which he was sentenced, because he did not want the name of his respectable parents in Croydon to be besmirched.

Marguerite Odell aka Margaret Chadwick Abell had parents too.

The 1921 census for 6 Rugby Mansions reveals her to have been plain Nellie Abell. She was a miner's daughter from Rotherham in Yorkshire and had been a schoolteacher before coming south to London to complete her own more lucrative education in the ways of the world. There was nowhere the twenties roared more than in Soho and the West End of London, and Nellie Abell in her furs and jewellery being gaily escorted around night clubs and fancy restaurants on the arms of appreciative gentlemen must have been the perfect mark and a tempting target for two young criminals.

* * * * * *

Chapter Note

1. Miss Edith Matts was almost certainly running a house of prostitution. At times she shared the address with up to four 'dressmakers'. As those who study occupations given in the census know, dressmaker and milliner were popular euphemisms for women who sold sex, and to find a group of them living at one address is a sure pointer. Walter Tarrant's occupation as a 'male house parlourmaid' in such an establishment provides a colourful addition to an account of his career!

CHAPTER NINE

BRIGHT YOUNG THINGS

It was a unique era. No one called them the Roaring Twenties until a journalist coined the phrase in 1933. For manufacturers and suppliers, the war had been very profitable. The so-called bright young things of the aristocracy and the wealthier classes felt they had never had it better. Many of them had been too young to fight, and some nursed a feeling of guilt that they had not experienced the horrors of war. Thousands of young women had cast off the shackles and morals of their parents and grandparents, skirts had shortened, while the generation that created the flapper also gave birth to gangsters, bootleggers and art deco.

As the war receded, people wanted a good time, many of them happy to pay for it tomorrow if they had to pay for it at all. Most women had the vote, and so did men over twenty-one. Enfranchised for the first time, Rosaline and Sidney put their names together on the electoral register for Cavendish Mansions.

Although he preferred the company of his men-friends, Sidney did enjoy the attention of women. Many of them were drawn to him, attaching themselves like human limpets in the night, prostitutes, actresses, chorus girls craving for gaiety, lost souls down on their luck for whom Sidney was a mascot. One of these was Freda Kempton, a twenty-one-year-old prostitute (or dancing instructress as she termed herself) whom he met in a night club. He described her as one of the most tragic little figures of modern Bohemia. He asked her to dance but got little response. He tried to joke her out of her depression but to no avail. She told him he was a 'nice boy' and assumed he wanted to talk 'business' but suggested he find a more congenial partner.

The source of her mood was revealed when 'a dapper little Chinaman entered, of sinister, even revolting appearance' and Freda grabbed the arm of the gallant Sidney for protection. She had taken a sniff of snow (cocaine), and the Chinese man, who strutted about the place as though he owned it, was her drug dealer and pimp. Sidney said he learned that night that scores of girls were in the grip of snow while others were slaves to opium and the hypodermic needle. If that was a new discovery to Sidney, he clearly hadn't been around as much as he made out. His female friend vanished, and he never saw her again. But he read about her in the newspapers.

She was found dead in her room in Westbourne Grove, Paddington, in March 1922 from an overdose of cocaine. Sidney said he read about her death the very next morning, which is almost certainly an invention aimed at elevating himself into the romantic role of one of the last people she met. But the tragedy of Freda Kempton's death was all too real and unromantic.

The Chinese man who had allegedly dealt her the drug was known as Brilliant Chang. He was proprietor of a Chinese restaurant in Regent Street. Billy Chang, to give him his real name, denied it at the inquest, saying she had asked him if sniffing cocaine could kill you. He had answered no, but if you dissolved it in water, it would. Freda Kempton had swallowed a tumbler full of water with over ten grains in it. The eminent Home Office pathologist Bernard Spilsbury (who the following year would be knighted and later would feature dramatically in Sidney's life) told the court that she had taken a more than fatal dose and that contrary to what Chang had told her, sniffing cocaine could also kill you. The verdict was suicide while temporarily insane.

Sidney never described in his life story sleeping with any woman. The one woman it is known that he did sleep with would be old enough to be his mother, of which more later. Then there was the young unnamed actress who he said led him towards his next escapade and prison sentence. Sidney didn't need anyone to lead him into prison; he was quite capable of getting there himself.

Sidney met her in Ciro's, a famous club and rendezvous for the smart set. He had twenty pounds in his pocket, and though she had once been an unknown, she was now quite famous and rehearsing for a new show. After a wild night dancing, they ended up with a crowd of others at the actress's flat where at ten in the morning they cooked bacon and eggs. She had to be at principals' rehearsals, so he took her there in a taxicab and later met her for lunch at the Old Cavour, a legendary and elegant gay hangout in Leicester Square. Not content with that social whirlwind, he rushed home for a change of clothes to take her out to dinner and finally a night at the Belgravia Hotel. He discovered she was married but separated from her husband and had no intention of being cited as a co-respondent. He abruptly told her that he had been called back to America on business and might have to leave at any time, and so the actress faded away. Not so the Belgravia Hotel in Victoria, where he deposited a parcel supposedly containing money and valuables with reception, one of the oldest hotel frauds in the book, and stayed there on his own for nine days, enjoying the high life.

'I was anxious to avoid romantic complications,' he explained, adding, 'I was determined to stick with my mother.'

At the end of his stay, he was about to walk out when he was presented with the bill. He admitted he had insufficient funds to pay and, asking them to correct some mistakes in the bill (mindful of the Sidney Fox philosophy that if you made problems, they were less likely to suspect you), told them to send it on to his parents in Hampstead. He then went home to his mother, leaving his luggage at the hotel. It seems astounding that hotels could have been so gullible, even in the days before credit cards and confirmed bookings. A week later, he wrote to the hotel asking them to forward the bill on to his bank. Instead, they wrote to Sidney, asking him to come and see them. He hadn't time, so he telephoned instead. It was presumably not until then that they made the decision to open the parcel that was sitting in their safe. It was full of scraps of paper. The suitcase, which was still sitting in his room, contained soiled linen.

Charged with obtaining credit by fraud at Westminster Police Court, this time as Sidney Harry Lane-Fox, he was given twelve months in Wandsworth Prison. It was his fourth custodial sentence. Rosaline, who had been staying back in Norfolk at the time, seeing family and friends, wrote a pleading letter to the Home Office, saying her son had no intention to defraud and that if he applied to her she would always pay his bills for him, adding for good effect her three sons lost to the war. Once again, Sidney's letter to the Home Office was equally disingenuous, claiming his money had been stolen which was the reason he couldn't pay the bill. Neither letter struck any ice, of course, and Sidney settled down to another year inside.

Prison life was hard, and as a good-looking young man who had difficulty hiding his sexual orientation, Sidney undoubtedly had his share of attention from other prisoners, much of it unwanted. During his time inside, Rosaline finally relocated from Cavendish Mansions. She'd had enough of the Tanthonys nosing about her business. She moved her possessions and those of Sidney to 8 Tavistock Terrace, much closer to where Jim Nelson lived.

Rosaline had antennae for friends who could put her up and had discovered that an old childhood friend, Emma Youngs from East Baddenham, a village close to Great Fransham, was married to a tram driver. It is uncanny how trains, trams and buses featured so strongly in Rosaline's life and among her acquaintances. She had chosen her first two lovers from the railway. She picked her third from the bus depot.

Perhaps she secretly desired to move in with Nelson, but he was a married man, and though conventions didn't always apply, Nelson may not have been willing to accommodate her errant son. And Rosaline had promised he would always have a home with her.

Upon his release, Sidney joined his mother at Tavistock Terrace, where one assumes the Youngs were not perturbed by his presence. Rosaline's pension of four shillings a week that she had been receiving since 1917 had been abolished and replaced with a pecuniary needs pension of ten shillings. It was still barely enough to live on. Sidney also had his small pension, which he supplemented in his usual manner. But at least they had a roof over their heads.

One of his first actions was to do something he knew would make her happy. She had always wanted to visit Cecil's grave in France, so Sidney went to the Graves Commission at Baker Street in London and elicited its location. A few days later, he received a letter containing a map and the information that it could be found as grave 16003 in the cemetery at Duisans. They wouldn't go there yet, but when they did, it would be an important milestone in Rosaline's life, and one that mattered deeply to both of them.

It was a small act of kindness. Sidney knew that his mother had loved the Cavendish Mansions flat and may well have felt guilty that he wasn't there at the end of their tenancy. If so, his next spell inside, this time for a crass and stupid crime, must have ratcheted up the guilt even more. Not for the first time, when she desperately needed her son, he wouldn't be there for her. On this occasion, it must have been agony for Sidney, but he brought it on himself.

He found employment as a valet with a General Beckett, an elderly army officer in Hammersmith. It was a wonderful house and a splendid situation, Sidney said, but once again he fell under the magic spell of a stray cheque book along with the beguiling sight of seventy-five pounds worth of jewellery. At the West London Police Court, where he was now becoming almost a regular, General Beckett stated, 'I'm afraid there is nothing good I can say about this man.'

Doctors found plenty to say, however, and a medical report was submitted to the court. It described him as irresponsible, feeble-minded and childish. They recommended that he be afforded 'some protection from his mental condition' otherwise he would continue on his downward path. It only stopped short of using the word insane.

The definition of insanity involved the perpetrator not knowing that what he was doing at the time was wrong. Sidney knew exactly what he was doing and that every time it was wrong. It was just that he couldn't help doing it.

Neither could the magistrates find anything good to say about him. Sidney obtained no benefit from the thefts and served another twelve months, this time between Wormwood Scrubs and Pentonville. Theft had become a behavioural addiction. Like many compulsive thieves and fraudsters, Sidney had developed a charming though deceptive personality with which to cover his tracks. But he never used violence or aggression. The only people he harmed were himself and Rosaline. If she had the power to stop him, she never used it. While he hunkered down inside, Rosaline was once again thrust upon the meagre government aid and the generosity of her friends.

It was too much for Emma and Fred Youngs, who didn't want Sidney coming back to their home. Rosaline had been an old friend and a welcome guest, but this was Sidney's fifth spell of incarceration in as many years, and it was clear he was never going to reform. Rosaline moved out, once again packing Sidney's possessions along with hers, and in anticipation of his release, found a place for them both at St John's Villas, near Archway Tube Station.

Then in September of that year, while Sidney was still inside, came the event that demonstrated to her how desperately alone she was. Jim Nelson fell ill. He was sixty-eight and suffering from heart disease. It is likely he had an attack, for he made his will just a few days before his death on 5 October 1924. Rosaline's only comfort was the knowledge that he had left her something in his will. She was in for an unpleasant surprise.

The value of his estate was £229, out of which he had left her only £25. The sum of £30 was left to his wife 'if living', something which Rosaline regarded as a gross insult after six years of caring for him. £20 had been left to another woman, to be paid at ten shillings a week. The whole of the residue was to be left to his executors, a fellow omnibus driver called George Lancaster and a friend, Leonard Burrows. If they could claim that Annie Nelson was dead, they would then legitimately pocket the thirty pounds he had left to his wife. Although £25 was a much-needed sum of money, Rosaline felt that, at the very least, the bequest to his wife should go to her.

It was a very badly worded will, at least from Rosaline's point of view. Probate could last for years in some cases, with costs eating up the estate, and this one was small enough to disappear in one mouthful overnight. It was, therefore, in the interests of Lancaster and Burrows to find her dead and find her quickly. It was in Rosaline's interests to dispute the will, which she did. Unfortunately for Rosaline, the matter was speedily resolved in the executors' favour. Probate was granted, and she received no more money. It was a bitter end to her relationship with her childhood friend.

Sidney came out of Pentonville in the spring of the following year, and on this occasion, it really did seem that he had managed to reform. He wrote in his life story that he 'hated the confinement, the restraint, the necessary hardship, and above all, the class of men I met'.

He promised her that it was the last time.

'I had many weeks of heart-breaking searching for work, until fortune shone on me again more than I deserved', he wrote.

He found a job with the Public Control Department of the London County Council as a clerk in the motor licensing department at County Hall. After a few months, they offered him a new job in their Education Section as assistant secretary at the School of Arts and Crafts in Southampton Row. At first it was only a temporary appointment, but they must have liked him because he was eventually offered a permanent position. He resolved to give up his wild nights. Rosaline was proud. It was evidence that he could do something worthwhile with his life, or so it seemed.

Fate had a habit of waiting around the corner for Sidney, and what happened to him was common to the experiences of many ex-convicts. Someone who knew him of old tipped off the assistant education officer, he was suspended pending enquiries and later received a letter enclosing a final cheque for his services.

Drastic action was needed. Rosaline had nothing to hold her in London now and determined to take Sidney away to somewhere he wasn't known and might stay out of trouble. They didn't move far at first. Shenfield, now a suburb of Brentford in Essex, was then a peaceful working village possessing much of the atmosphere of Great Fransham, though with easy rail connections to London.

For four months, they lodged with an elderly lady called Emily Sinclair in a villa in Alexandra Road. Her husband had been a corn dealer, and two of her sons were saddlers. She was eighty-six and known as Pridie to her family and soon also to Rosaline and Sidney, who became great friends. She became fond of them, particularly of Sidney, who she regarded as no more than a charming rogue. They liked her so much that they came back later in the year and spent a further three months.

If Rosaline thought that the country air might keep Sidney away from temptation, she was mistaken. The rail links were good, and there was an excellent connection to Liverpool Street Station. But at least he would come home to her most nights, even if every night was too much to ask for.

It is easy to sometimes lose sight of the fact there was one crime she couldn't keep Sidney from, and that was his homosexual relationships, punishable by two years in prison. Those were largely with older men, mostly for money, sometimes as direct payments, often as gifts and friendly loans. Whether he or she was aware of it or not, he had sought father figures all his life, from Gerald Hamilton to army officers like Percy Holland. Those were men who took enormous risks to be with Sidney as well. The illegitimate child, derided at school for having no proper father other than the one he shared with a school friend, needed such men in his life.

If there had been a mystery about Rosaline's income when she was younger, there was none about Sidney's. Rosaline had to know about the prostitution. She could pretend that his male friendships were just that, but the inherent dangers must have given her many sleepless nights. Where else was the money coming from? She was sixty-one, had been a ravishingly beautiful country girl in her youth, and still had the features she had passed on to Sidney, looks which now helped her son to become the breadwinner of the family. Photographs of Rosaline show a face that beams with health. But they are deceptive, like the woman herself. She was starting to become frail and to shake. She had developed *paralysis agitans*, now better known as Parkinson's Disease. She needed her younger son more than ever as she stared old age and infirmity in the face.

Sidney would not let her down. He would make more friends, meet more powerful and influential people who would help both of them on their way through life. He needed them just as much as he needed his mother.

Waiting in the wings was a man of great eminence, a political figure and a potential danger to Sidney, who was already sowing the seeds of his own destruction.

* * * * * *

CHAPTER TEN

A LICENTIOUS LORD

Sidney came into possession of a motorcycle. It cost him dearly when he was riding through Esher in Surrey and collided with a car driven by the splendidly named Charles Lawless Redcliffe Barrett and broke his leg. The two of them slowed up to allow a lorry to turn into a side road, and each accused the other of being on the wrong side at the time of the impact. Sidney took him to court at the Kings Bench division in London, saying that at the time of the collision he was earning £350 a year and had lost his employment—which employment is not mentioned—and that his leg had become one inch shorter because of the accident. He lost the case and was obliged to pay damages, for which he was subsequently made bankrupt. During the court case, he stayed with Lupson, and the two of them spent their evenings around the old gay haunts.

It was at Lupson's flat that Sidney was introduced to Gordon Campbell. Seven years his senior, Campbell was a salesman and departmental manager for a firm of silk and cotton merchants, Cox and Edwards in Old Cavendish Street, a company which also specialised in gauzes, velvets, haberdashery and, rather oddly, British and foreign cigars. He had served both in the Navy and the Royal Air Force and came from a musical and theatrical family. This was manna to Sidney, and they hit it off straight away.

Campbell's mother appears to have ignored the advice about not putting one's daughter on the stage. Campbell had three sisters, Madge, Marie and Rose, all of them at one time young aspiring actresses. Madge had the brightest theatrical career ahead of her. She toured with John Tiller, the producer who had a lightbulb moment of discovery when he created The Tiller Girls. Previously, dancers had looked messy and uncoordinated, and his brainwave was to make them link arms. Madge impressed audiences wherever she went, and there is no doubt the name of Madge Campbell might have become famous had she not married the nephew of the Chief Justice of New South Wales and moved to Australia.

Gordon Campbell's industriousness had been noted by his employers, and he was on his way to becoming a well-off merchant in the firm, possessing something Sidney knew he would never have, a job for life. Sidney was a somewhat risky social waif to know for a man in Campbell's position, but from their first meeting, Campbell became a regular companion, always ready to advance Sidney money. And with bankruptcy hanging over him, two rooms in Shenfield to pay for, and his mother to support, Sidney needed cash.

He, Lupson and Campbell would remain long-lasting friends until it was no longer practical for them to do so.

They toured pubs, went to the theatre, met for lunch, and stayed overnight with one another. They were like the three musketeers, one for all and all for one. There was little either of them would not do for Sidney. Financial support apart, they gave him a much-needed stability. He provided them with the wicked pleasure of his company, and not just for sex. 'The kid' had drifted into their domain, and he would stick there loyally. It is quite possible both of them were in love with him.

How he then strayed into the promiscuous circle of William Lygon, 7th Earl Beauchamp, former governor of New South Wales and leader of the Liberal Party in the House of Lords, is anyone's guess but not hard to imagine. He certainly did not pick the earl's name out of Debrett's with a pin. When it came to 'notorious sodomites', Beauchamp's name was up there at the top of the list and among his many London associates were actors and theatrical hangers-on like Sidney.

At the tender age of twenty-eight, the young Earl Beauchamp had been euphemistically described in the Australian press as 'not a marrying man'. Neither was he a sportsman, a quality the Australians liked to see in their governors, preferring instead the company of younger male artistic souls. That, along with his youth, was constantly brought up as a detriment to his abilities, one acerbic journalist commenting that as his skin was as smooth as a duck egg, he would have no need of a shaving bowl at Government House. Almost from the moment of his appointment, there were rumours that he did not take to the tough life in the Antipodes and wished to resign, which he did a year later. He also annoyed residents of the colony by commenting on their lack of democracy. The democratic and smooth-skinned earl returned to England, where he joined the Liberal Party and confounded expectations by marrying. His wife, Lady Lettice, the daughter of Victor Grosvenor, Earl Grosvenor, bore him seven children.

By the time Sidney crossed his path, he was Liberal leader in the Upper House, in his early fifties, and hiding in not very plain sight the activities which were to be his undoing. Those may have given rise to mere suspicion in the colony, but in England it was an open secret in certain quarters that he not only employed his footmen according to their sexual persuasions but buggered his favourites in the garage of his town house in Belgravia Square. As Lord Warden of the Cinque Ports, a ceremonial title bestowed on him by his close friend the King, he also had the official use of Walmer Castle in Kent. Tales circulated about Beauchamp's indiscretions at dinners and banquets where he would whisper romantically in his servants' ears or stroke their bottoms. He also liked what we would call today rough trade, local lads from the Kentish ports, unemployed youths and young fishermen, and was once spotted with a boy in the not quite so noble surrounds of the Elephant and Castle public baths.

Sidney, who could assume a new name or a title as frequently as he changed his shirt, depending on the company and the course he intended to navigate, adopted the name of Wilson Fox. Years later when he was down on his luck, 'Mr Wilson Fox' would brazenly turn up on the doorstep of his one-time benefactor's Belgravia home looking for 'funds', a gentle reminder of their previous association. This would come to the attention of the police. For the moment, however, in these carefree days, Sidney would not have missed out on the opportunity to become a guest at one of the notorious and eccentric revels which went on at the castle.

A flavour of those gatherings can be taken from an account left by the society hostess and author Christabel Aberconway, who boasted that her first friend was Oscar Wilde, whose plump white finger she had held in her tiny hand while still in her pram. She had been a guest at Walmer Castle along with the actor Ernest Thesiger, whom she had encountered bare-chested and lounging about in a string of pearls by the earl's tennis court. Thesiger, whose hobby was embroidery, that year appeared in drag on stage in Noel Coward's *On With The Dance*. She was also introduced to several other young male party guests, one of whom Earl Beauchamp introduced as his tennis coach. She immediately picked up a racquet and asked him to send her some difficult serves. The tennis coach may have boasted many talents, but putting a ball over the net was not one of them.

On that particular occasion, Aberconway was accompanied by a fellow guest who was not so open-minded. Sir William Jowitt was a Liberal MP and lawyer who a few years later would become Attorney General under a minority Labour government. His would be a name with which Sidney would one day have to reckon.

Earl Beauchamp had his own reckoning ahead. Sidney would not be the source of his downfall, as he was Colonel Holland's, but his association with Beauchamp would eventually contribute to his own. The earl's wife was the sister of the womanising and intensely homophobic Duke of Westminster, who would become Beauchamp's nemesis just as the Marquis of

Queensberry was Oscar Wilde's. Lady Lettice was mainly entrenched at Madresfield, a house which had once hosted Evelyn Waugh and inspired him to write *Brideshead Revisited*. She knew nothing of her husband's sex life, or so it was said. When told by her brother of her husband's proclivities, she is reputed to have thought he was referring to her husband being a bugler or a burglar, while the King, on being informed, remarked bluntly of his great friend, 'I thought these people shot themselves?' (1)

If Rosaline Fox thought that taking Sidney away from London would keep him out of trouble, she did not know the half of it. This was the life her son craved, and these were the kind of people in whose company he felt most comfortable. The types he met in prison could not hold their own in situations like this. The upper classes were untouchable, and so long as he was one of them, he thought, so was he. In truth, he wasn't one of them and never would be. He was an interloper. When Earl Beauchamp became fed up with him, he would be cast out. In *De Profundis* in 1905, Wilde coined the phrase 'sleeping with panthers'. Earl Beauchamp would find more dangerous and exciting creatures with whom to share his bed.

Meanwhile it became time for Rosaline and Sidney to leave Pridie Sinclair and move on. Rosaline had been happy in Shenfield, like a little girl again, surrounded by farm animals and the kind of simple country folk with whom she had grown up. Pridie had more opportunities than most to watch the way they behaved together. They were more like husband and wife, she thought. They played together and indulged in the little games that lovers enjoyed. Sidney might not always be by her side, but when he was, he would bring her things. He would see her all right. They were inseparable.

William Fox, who two years earlier had been promoted to charge nurse at Ewell, moved to Hampshire, where he took a better job as a monitor in the newly opened Alexandra Hospital at Cosham near Portsmouth, set up by the Ministry of Pensions to care for ex-soldiers afflicted with disabilities, nervous and mental complaints. Married quarters were also provided. It meant that Rosaline would have much further to travel now if she wanted to see her only granddaughter. That affected her decision as to where to move next, and she settled on Southsea. She had always wanted to live by the coast. Sidney might find a proper job and would be further away from the criminal temptations of London. So she thought.

Sidney acceded to her request, though not through any desire to be nearer to his brother. He, too, felt that he needed a change. With a solemn promise to invite Alfred Lupson and Gordon Campbell down when they were settled, Sidney joined Rosaline in packing up their possessions, putting some in storage, and planning a new start on the south coast.

Their stay in Southsea worked out very differently from how either of them imagined. The darkest and strangest chapter in their lives was yet to unfold. It would involve a remarkable series of incidents that shine a whole new light on the relationship between mother and son, and introduce a cast of characters so unbelievable in their gullibility and complicity that a novelist wouldn't even dare to invent it.

It is time to meet an Australian lady who was about to have the holiday romance from hell.

* * * * * *

Chapter Note

1. It was not given to many people in their lifetimes to meet someone who would later become immortalised in fiction, let alone two, but such a privilege dropped in Sidney's lap. As we have seen, Gerald Hamilton, Sidney's mentor and many other things besides, would become the chastisement-loving Mr Norris in Isherwood's *Mr Norris Changes Trains*. In getting to know Earl Beauchamp, Sidney found himself in the company of the man now widely believed to be the original model for Lord Marchmain in *Brideshead Revisited*. Any similarity between the dour, straight Lord Marchmain of fiction and the vivacious, party-loving earl was illusory, based on little more than that both ended up in exile, and each adopted Venice as his favourite city. Evelyn Waugh attended Oxford with Beauchamp's son, Hugh Lygon, himself gay and on whom he would base the louche, drunken and tragic Sebastian Flyte.

CHAPTER ELEVEN

ENTER MRS MORSE

Southsea, in the interwar years, had drifted out of fashion but was still a popular seaside resort, with a vast expanse of common that stretched from Clarence Pier to Southsea Castle, which gave the town its name. It was a place with all the usual entertainments, pier shows, golf and beaches, while embraced by Portsmouth, which was unmistakably a military town and a naval port.

It was not long before Sidney made connections or renewed those he had forged in London. He could always track down an older army officer to whom he could turn for a quick favour. One of those was Captain Eustace Bartrip, Royal Artillery, who lived on Lumps Fort, a defence structure that had been decommissioned after the Great War. Sidney approached him for help in finding a job in Portsmouth. It was a town he wasn't known in, so both mother and son hoped that this time his past might not catch up with him. Sidney thought it best not to go into banking, which was a wise choice, but something had set him on the notion of selling insurance. Captain Bartrip knew just the fellow to help.

Major William Henry Powell DSO was the local branch manager of the Gresham Insurance Company, which was based in London. He was a Portsmouth man, born and bred, and had the distinction of being the first ranking officer to win the Distinguished Service Order in the war. Having won his spurs in the army, he set upon winning his spurs in civic duties, one of those by helping ex-servicemen whom he felt Portsmouth had let down badly.

When Sidney walked into his office and talked about his military career, such as it was, Major Powell saw a well-dressed, well-spoken and persuasive young man who could turn his hand to selling insurance as easily as falling off a log. He decided to take him on, offering him a temporary job to start with, but if he proved successful, Major Powell said he would make the job permanent. Sidney had heard that before. But he must have found a niche because for the first few months, he brought in business that delighted his employer. Selling insurance was a job for which Sidney's talents had clearly been developed.

Rosaline, meanwhile, was making new friends of her own. Amid a fever of later inaccurate speculation and sensational headlines in Australia, the ironically named periodical *Sydney Truth* would claim that Sidney met Charlotte Morse first at a wild party and took her home to meet his mother at 26 Cavendish Mansions, which, for good measure, they occupied on the proceeds of a drugs deal. The Foxes had left Cavendish Mansions long before Mrs Morse came on the scene. The promenade at Southsea, however, with its benches looking out across the sparkling sea, was a perfect place for two unaccompanied ladies to fall into conversation.

Her father was a wealthy merchant in Sydney. She had married George Alfred Graham Morse, a captain with the Shire Line, which sailed mainly to India and the Far East in Shanghai, and had followed him around, living in Hong Kong for a while. They had two sons, Reginald and George, whom they had brought to England in 1923 to put into a boarding school in Surrey. Charlotte and her husband were now separated owing to her extravagant living, though there were almost certainly other reasons for the break-up of the marriage, one being Charlotte's temperament as a fun-seeking, freedom-loving middle-aged woman, now fifty-three, no longer interested in being a dutiful wife and more inclined to play the role of a merry widow. Captain Morse allowed her thirty pounds a month; her father, George Morgan, allowed her fifty. Out of this, she was under an obligation to provide for the boys, but Charlotte was more interested in providing for herself. Besides, her father would always pay up when needed. He had been obliged once already to send a hundred pounds to take care of unpaid bills.

When in England, Captain Morse lived at his permanent address in Primrose Hill, London. He was a member of the prestigious Golfers Club, which had its headquarters at Whitehall Court overlooking the Thames, the historic city landmark that now houses the National Liberal Club and the Royal Horseguards Hotel. As such, he was able to make use of residential facilities, which Charlotte as a lady golfer (they had their own club) and their sons were also able to use. This may have given Sidney and Rosaline the false impression that she was far wealthier than she appeared and that she owned significant property.

Captain Morse had now sailed back to the Far East. His final Southsea address, recorded on the passenger list of the Blue Funnel Liner *Ascanius,* was a house called Mariston. Mariners are notoriously superstitious. Captain Morse must have known that the *Mariston* was the name of a steamer which had been sunk by a U-boat torpedo. Every man on board except one was picked screaming off the wreckage by a frenzy of sharks. Even the U-boat commander could not bear to watch, put up the hatch and sailed away. Captain Morse made it safely to China, but his wife back in England was set on a course for treacherous waters.

On the face of it, Rosaline Fox and Charlotte Morse had nothing in common. Charlotte was worldly and well provided for. Rosaline was still on a pension of ten shillings a week and had little to her name, though she liked to give the impression of being well off. There is little doubt, however, that Charlotte would not have befriended Rosaline for long if it hadn't been for meeting her son. All the evidence points to the fact she groomed Rosaline to get close to Sidney.

Charlotte Morse was old enough to be his mother, but from the moment they were introduced, she became intrigued by him. She wrote to her two friends in Hampstead, maiden sisters Gertrude and Lilian Weston, who ran a dress shop in Oxford Street, to tell of the 'nice fascinating young man' she had met in Southsea. Later, the nice fascinating young man would be described as a 'very nice boyfriend'. The sharks were gathering, though Charlotte clearly had man-eating capacities herself.

In every account of this part of the story, it has been assumed that Sidney sidelined his homosexual desires to seduce the lady and separate her from her money. In the *Notable British Trials* series, the crime writer Frynn Tennyson Jesse, who penned the excellent introduction to Sidney's trial, lays the seduction firmly at Sidney's door, even going so far as to say he made violent love to her to achieve those ends. Jesse fails to account for how she might have acquired that intimate bedroom knowledge, but Sidney and Rosaline saw Charlotte almost certainly as a source of much-needed funds. Charlotte Morse was as much to blame, thrusting her hands into a fire that she must have known was going to burn her. She was, after all, still a married woman.

Rosaline became the recipient of gifts and loans, which Sidney would later refer to as an income, while he benefitted from the fact she was obsessed with him and was willing to pay for her, and his, pleasures. All three eventually moved into a flat together at 31 Clarence Parade, for which Charlotte paid the rent. Facing across the common to the sea, Clarence Parade was one of the best addresses in Southsea.

Sidney and Rosaline had both been kept by men. This was the first time they had been kept jointly by a woman, and Sidney wasn't going to deny his mother a piece of the action. Charlotte may not have been initially aware of Sidney's homosexuality, but in a short time she must have discovered it and seen it not as an impediment. Hundreds of women have fallen in love with gay men and believed themselves capable of rising to the challenge and converting them. Given time, she thought, Sidney would come round to her. And even if he didn't, for his part, he was always prepared to sleep with anybody for money, man or woman. If Sidney needed any advice on how to keep an older woman satisfied and on side, he only had his mother to ask.

In his life story, Sidney gave a less oedipal and simpler impression of their relationship:

'I think mother must have told her something of her worry concerning me, for I knew it was only to get me away from London, and the possible temptations there, that they suggested taking a boarding house in the Southsea district. Gladly I fell in with the idea... Mrs Morse was extremely kind to me during the time we were there. She had a son of her own and I suppose felt a sort of motherly attraction for Sidney Fox. Often we went long walks together, and Mrs Morse would talk to me just as a mother might. I grew to like and respect her. Without her I do not know what we should have done at times, she was generosity itself.'

That generosity was to take some remarkable turns in the course of the year.

Major Powell was delighted with the business Sidney brought in. He and his wife came to tea with Sidney and his mother and began to meet them regularly. On one occasion, they were invited to take tea with Mrs Morse as well. It is tempting to picture the genteel scene of the three ladies, one the dutiful wife of a local businessman, one a loquacious Australian matriarch with a longing for sexual adventure, and the quieter and more reserved Rosaline Fox who enjoyed her whisky and soda, all daintily eating their scones and jam and drinking tea out of china cups while Major Powell and Sidney discussed insurance business. Major Powell would note that Rosaline was fond of her whisky. She seemed unsteady on her legs and would often fall down, more a symptom of her developing condition.

On the August Bank Holiday, Sidney invited Gordon Campbell to come down and stay with them at Clarence Parade. Campbell brought with him for the holiday a young friend called Rowland Brake. He also introduced Sidney to a single male friend Leslie Greenfield who had been in the RAF with him and who lived on the Isle of Wight with his father, running a building and contracting business. This little network of male companions was well supplemented by Brake, who had the kind of background Sidney envied, an education at the Royal Latin School in Buckingham, one of the most prestigious grammar schools in the country, and a job as an engineer with the National Telephone Company

There was an element of pairing off as they went out on the town, Sidney keeping company with the older Campbell, while Greenfield spent more time with the good-looking and incredibly well-spoken Brake. They all ended up at Clarence Parade, having tea with Rosaline Fox. Mrs Morse appears not to have been there that day for she was spending the holiday with her sons in London. There is no doubt she would have revelled in the company of so many young gay men.

Leslie Greenfield would soon have the pleasure of meeting her on a number of occasions, one in circumstances that would turn out to be highly compromising to both his intelligence and straight reputation. For as the summer wore on, it was more and more apparent to anyone who had eyes to see that Mrs Morse not only looked on Sidney as a surrogate son but as a lover. Sidney was starting to call her his aunt. She would think nothing of sitting in his room in her nightdress, talking for hours.

Sidney had become good friends with Greenfield, and they met up regularly for drinks in Portsmouth pubs, where no doubt sailors proved an occasional diversion. Sidney saw Greenfield as an excellent target for insurance selling. Greenfield bought a Standard car for £150, and Sidney persuaded him to insure it for £175 through the Gresham. He paid Sidney a first premium and, at the same time, took out a life insurance policy for £500 with profits, for which he paid one premium only before letting it lapse. Sidney then tried to get him to insure his life against accident, but in spite of introducing him to Major Powell, no other policies came to fruition.

Sidney wasn't finished with Leslie Greenfield.

If Rosaline and Mrs Morse had pooled normal motherly resources and kept their boy on the straight and narrow path he seemed to have found in Southsea, things might have worked out differently, but Sidney's compulsive lying and need for fantasy in his life came rushing up on the tide, unstoppable even when it threatened to demolish the castle he had built for himself. Pleased with his progress, Major Powell contacted the head office in London and said he would like to offer Sidney a permanent position, but now, alas, references were required. Sidney said he had worked for the Bank of England as a clerk and that they would give him a good reference. He hadn't, and they didn't.

Sidney was doing what he always did, kicking the sandcastle to bits, consigning it to oblivion. His record over the summer was excellent, and Major Powell might just have given him a sporting chance, so good had their relationship become. Head Office was, of course, a different thing. Sidney had lied and was obliged to go.

No matter, he proudly told Major Powell that he had been offered a job as personal secretary to Lord Glentanar of the Coats Threads family dynasty who had an estate in Scotland. This admission may have surprised Major Powell, but it would not surprise anyone who knew Sidney, who seemed to pick up members of the House of Lords like seashells. Thomas Coats, 2nd Baron Glentanar, was that very month in Cowes on the Isle of Wight, just across the water, sailing his 14ft dinghy in the Prince of Wales Cup. He was a close friend of Lord Lathom, Sidney's generous theatrical companion who had taken him to so many first nights and stage parties. The two aristocrats, Glentanar and Lathom, were practically tipped out of the same mould.

Known as the Singing Peer because of his rich baritone voice, Glentanar was the richest man in Scotland. He had converted the ballroom of his house on Deeside into what was described as the finest private theatre in the country. Like Lord Lathom, he was not only a landowner but a playwright and performed in many of his own productions. He owned a London home in Berkeley Square, with Italian works of art, a Louis Seize ballroom, and suites with sunken marble baths for visitors. He was only a few years older than Sidney, having come into his four-million-pound fortune at the age of twenty-five.

The only gossip about one of the most eligible bachelors in the country was to which lucky lady he would hand his heart and his fortune. He eventually gave it to the Norwegian heiress of a shipping line, with whom he would have one daughter. Lord Glentanar was an enthusiastic supporter of the Scout movement and would take Baden Powell, a close friend, on his grand yacht around the Western Isles to inspect the more isolated troops of Scottish scouts.

Major Powell was dismayed, but he wished Sidney well and they parted company.

Sidney's wonderful sounding job as personal secretary to Lord Glentanar did not materialise. The offer may have been entirely or partly in Sidney's imagination or put to him in a moment of reckless bonhomie. Or just maybe Glentanar looked at his charts and, unlike Charlotte Morse, chose to avoid dangerous currents.

Meanwhile, Mrs Morse was still extolling Sidney's virtues to her friends, the Weston sisters. When they met Sidney, they were not quite so enamoured. On the occasions Mrs Morse's two sons Reginald and George were invited down, Gertrude and Lilian would be invited too, and were expected to take the boys to the theatre so Charlotte Morse could be alone with Sidney. Gertrude was so angry at the situation she could see developing—after all, Rosaline Fox seemed to all intents and purposes to be part of the equation—that she told Reginald he should remonstrate with his mother. Reginald did. Charlotte Morse told him to mind his own business.

It is difficult to shy away completely from the thought that Rosaline might have been complicit in what happened next, for the circumstances surrounding the making of Charlotte Morse's will and the alleged attempt to take her life were peculiar in the extreme.

* * * * * *

CHAPTER TWELVE

THE INCIDENT OF THE GAS TAP IN THE NIGHT-TIME

In the autumn of that year, Charlotte Morse committed the ultimate act of devotion to her Sidney—or folly, depending on which way one looks at it—and left him everything she owned in her will. She added a clause requesting that if she should die before paying back to Sidney the five thousand pounds she had borrowed from him, her father in New South Wales was immediately obliged to take care of the debt. Leaving aside the fact that Sidney did not have, or ever did have, five thousand pounds to lend anybody, we need to step back and see how this remarkable document, and others, came about.

The parties left Clarence Parade, and like an itinerant band, Sidney, Rosaline and Mrs Morse moved lodgings *en masse* twice. First they took apartments in a boarding house run by a Mrs Lester, who lived with her son, Albert, a tailor. One day—he said it was a date between 15 October and 29 October 1927—Albert was summoned to the sitting room. Waiting for him were Sidney, Mrs Morse and another young man who he did not know, probably Greenfield. He was not quite clear if Rosaline Fox was in the room, but recounting the incident he 'thought it probable that she was there'.

Either Sidney or Mrs Morse, he couldn't remember which, asked him to witness a will. Two years later, he was shown the same will and a promissory note, basically an IOU, and agreed that they both appeared to bear his signature, but that he could not remember signing either of them. The odd thing about the promissory note was its date, 1 October. Albert said he didn't know any of the parties at that time. They hadn't arrived at his mother's house until the middle of the month.

Mrs Morse and the unknown young man then signed the documents. Everyone was talking. Albert couldn't remember what about. Of only one thing he was certain, he signed them without reading them. At that point, Albert left the room. A few days later, Rosaline, Sidney and Mrs Morse moved to their third furnished Southsea address, 2 St Helens Towers in Clarendon Road.

This ill-fated address, just at the back of Clarence Parade, was not as grand as the name suggested. The towers referred only to a basement flat, a ground floor, and a top or second-floor flat. But they were substantial, each with five rooms and kitchen and bathroom. Sidney chose as his bedroom that which had belonged to the proprietress, Mrs Hilda Fleming, who showed him round and apparently told him there was a gas tap behind a chest of drawers which, if moved carelessly, could accidentally turn the tap on. This warning having been firmly implanted in Sidney's mind, he, his mother and Mrs Morse said they intended to stay there for three months. As is natural with landladies renting their houses to strangers, Mrs Fleming was eager to know about their past, and Sidney, as he did with everyone, relished the opportunity to spin the story that he had served in the Royal Flying Corps.

The fifty-three-year-old Mrs Fleming had a colourful past herself. She was of an old British colonial family in the West Indies and had been born in Trinidad. She had married an English doctor, Charles Jenner Parson who, after discovering his first wife's adultery on numerous voyages around the Indian Ocean, had just been through an acrimonious divorce. Two years later, as the new Mr and Mrs Parson, they went to live on the volcanic island of St Vincent in the Caribbean, where they had a son. As Mrs Fleming was proud to boast, Charles Hugh Beresford Jenner Parson had become a flight sub-lieutenant with the Royal Navy. He had been mentioned in despatches for distinguished and gallant services at Dunkirk. Three years after his birth, she lost her husband in Trinidad, and two years after that, La Soufriere volcano erupted on St Vincent killing thousands.

Concluding what sounded like a Somerset Maugham novel, Hilda took for her second husband a major in the Royal Army Medical Corps before travelling to England and taking up the profession of seaside landlady.

It was a Sunday, shortly after they had settled in at St Helen's Towers, when Leslie Greenfield joined Sidney, his mother and Charlotte Morse at their new address to go for a drive to Lyndhurst in Hampshire in Sidney's recently acquired Morris car. Before the happy excursion, they had lunch whereupon Sidney brought some papers into the room.

This time, Rosaline, Mrs Morse and Hilda Fleming were all present, according to Greenfield. Sidney told his friend he would like him to sign some papers and that he could read them if he liked, but as they were in a hurry to set out on their jaunt, it wouldn't be necessary. To the best of his recollection, Greenfield thought he heard Sidney say they were insurance policies. He had no idea who or what the insurance was for, a remarkable lack of interest considering Sidney had already sold him car insurance.

He signed the papers first, then Mrs Morse, then Hilda Fleming. Why Hilda Fleming should have been brought into the room was not explained. Later on, the landlady denied ever being there or ever meeting Mrs Morse. Sidney kept reminding him they were in a hurry to get out, so he didn't read any of the papers. Just like Lester, Greenfield, two years later, would be shown both documents and would agree that the signatures were his. They all then piled into the car (except Hilda Fleming), and Sidney drove them to the New Forest, where they spent a lovely Sunday afternoon. Greenfield paid for the tea.

The upshot of these cosy gatherings was the IOU dated 1 October from Charlotte Morse, which stated simply, 'On demand I promise to pay Mr Sidney Harry Fox the sum of five thousand pounds for value received, together with interest at the rate of six per cent, payable at St. Helen's Towers, Southsea, Hants'.

The second was a will dated 27 October, appointing Sidney as her sole executor and beneficiary, which went on to remind her father that, should he have mislaid or ignored the IOU or thrown it in the bin, 'in the event of my death, before I have paid the said Sidney Harry Fox the sum of five thousand pounds which I borrowed from him, I wish my father George Morgan, Esq., Merchant and Importer of 211 Clarence Street, Sydney, Australia, to pay the said Sidney Harry Fox this sum together with interest as specified on the promissory note I have duly signed'.

Both were clearly designed to defraud Charlotte's father. Charlotte Morse may have been lovestruck, but she wasn't stupid. She would have taken great care with a will which revoked all previous ones, considering she had two sons. At what point she decided to conspire with Sidney in a criminal enterprise can only be guessed at, but it probably had its genesis when they were at Clarence Parade and during their long walks together.

If her father made good on the IOU, Sidney and Rosaline would be richer than they had ever been in their lives, and Charlotte would almost certainly have been in for a cut. The will, however, depended on Charlotte dying before Sidney could get the money. She was a strong, healthy woman who in fact would live for another twenty-six years. This does not seem to have alarmed her, neither does it appear to have bothered her that Sidney had also insured her life.

The third document to come out of the signings was an insurance policy by which Sidney would benefit if she died. Sidney had worked for Major Powell long enough to know a thing or two about insurance. It was perfectly legal then to insure the life of, and benefit from, the death of someone to whom you weren't related. The insured party could be someone who was almost a total stranger, the local shopkeeper, the man who drove the Clapham omnibus, just so long as you got their signature on the proposal form and paid the premiums. It was a passport to murder.

By a strange coincidence, Reginald Morse, Charlotte's son, was also working as a clerk for an insurance company in London at the time. She did not ask his advice, neither did Sidney go through Major Powell and the Gresham. It was done through a separate agency. Many years later, back in Australia, Reginald would give his version of what happened, the only version that really has any currency. He said his mother had been persuaded by Sidney to take out a policy for a hundred pounds. When Reginald went to the company, he learned to his astonishment that the sum was actually six thousand pounds. Reginald and the company manager agreed that the '1' had been turned into a '6' and a nought had been added. The policy had been immediately cancelled.

The will, the promissory note and the insurance proposal had the stamp of Sidney all over them.

Christmas intervened, and as it does elsewhere in the world, normal life, if it could be so described at St Helen's Towers, was put on hold. Sidney and his mother went to spend it with William in his married quarters at the Alexandra Hospital in Cosham, while Charlotte spent it with her sons in London.

Christmas with the Foxes was not a success. Rosaline enjoyed the company of her granddaughter Marjorie, but William despised his brother and put up with him only for the sake of his wife. He found his mother difficult to manage and thought she was depressed. He observed, too, that she was growing feeble and prone to falling, and he didn't want to be responsible for her. When Sidney left her there and went off to do what Sidney always did, disappearing up to London, William went to the Gresham Insurance Company looking for him. He wanted Sidney to take her away. He learned only then that Major Powell had dispensed with Sidney's services. It was a relief for all of them when Christmas was finally over.

Entrenched back at St Helen's Towers for the final month of their tenancy, January 1928, they continued to be visited by Mrs Morse's two sons. One night George, the younger boy, was down on his own. He was fourteen and still at boarding school at that time. The Weston sisters were not around to take him to the theatre and get him out of the way for the evening, so the party had to behave with decorum.

Sidney could not be expected to occupy the same bed as the boy's mother, so it was arranged that out of propriety, George would sleep in the double bed with Sidney while Charlotte occupied Sidney's bedroom. What was said to occur that night is a matter of some controversy.

At first, there was only the word of young George. He alleged that during the night, Sidney got up and went into his own bedroom where Mrs Morse was sleeping and tried to give her some drink and that there was an altercation owing to the fact that he wouldn't leave her room. This sounds logical, as she would not have wanted her younger son to get a hint of what was going on. His brother Reginald might have told him, but that was different from letting him see it with his own eyes. Charlotte was a lot of things, but she still had a mother's instinct. Sidney eventually left the room and climbed back into bed with George.

Some time later, Charlotte Morse woke up and smelt gas in the bedroom. She felt as though she had been poisoned and raised the alarm, getting everybody out of bed. Sidney was first on the scene. Windows were thrust open to let the gas out. It is not clear who found the source, but it was Sidney's bedroom she was sleeping in, and the gas tap behind the chest of drawers had somehow become turned on, as Mrs Fleming had very conveniently warned could happen.

This incident subsequently has gone down in the mythology of the case as Sidney's first attempt to commit murder. Years later, Sidney would admit to a friend and journalist that the incident did occur but that he was indignant at the suggestion he was responsible. (1)

If Charlotte's father wasn't going to make good on the fraudulent demand for five thousand pounds, then there was her will and a large insurance policy as motive. But there are a number of very odd features. Did Sidney really go back into her room after she had told him to get out, move the heavy piece of furniture, satisfy himself that the gas tap was on, and then go back to bed and lie awake and wait for her to die? Unless a room was well sealed off, the gas would seep out and affect other rooms in the household, including his mother's and his own, with the added risk of blowing them all off the face of the earth.

No investigation was ever made at the time, so we do not know if there was a gas fire in Sidney's bedroom where Mrs Morse was sleeping or how draughty the flat was. She was an Australian used to a very different climate than that normally encountered on the south coast of England in winter, so it would be reasonable to assume if there was, she would have it on. Gas jets were very commonly used for lighting at that time, so it is probable that this was the source. Coal gas was very different from the natural gas we use today. It had a pungent and penetrating odour, and its carbon monoxide content could kill. A recent report into its dangers highlighted nearly two hundred cases of accidental death as well as over a thousand suicides. It found that unthinking consumers made mistakes due to carelessness and that most of those who came to grief absent-mindedly confused the handling of their taps. Tubes, pipes and meters were sometimes defective, and types of old-fashioned chandeliers were particularly dangerous.

It will never be known exactly what happened that night. The gas luckily was not ignited, but suspicions were, though not until a few weeks later when the domestic situation had changed considerably.

It has generally been assumed that the incident ended the relationship between Sidney and Charlotte, but this was not the case. Far from it, Charlotte Morse had invested far too much time and passion in the relationship and wasn't easily going to believe that Sidney intended to kill her. Their affair, however, had not much longer to run. Other factors would determine her course of action.

Throughout the signings and the episode of the gas tap, Rosaline remains the silent partner. Inscrutable, her cherubic smiling face turned to the sea, a whisky and soda in her hand, she would have known that, in spite of what might or might not be happening in their bedroom, her son would never desert her for Charlotte Morse. He was her insurance, and she didn't need any dodgy policy to confirm that.

There is an astonishing irony in the fact that it would be in another bedroom, in another town, that a gas fire in front of which she herself was sitting would play its part in a second mysterious drama.

* * * * * *

Chapter Note

1. *The Melbourne Argus*, 31 March 1930. The friend was almost certainly Adelaide Foster, a journalist and crime writer who got to know Sidney well and visited him frequently. See Chapter 23.

Sidney Harry Fox. Image courtesy of National Archives.

Rosaline Fox. Image courtesy of Margate Museum.

Rosaline and Sidney, a seaside studio portrait
circa 1927. Image courtesy of Margate Museum.

The jetty at Margate showing the
Metropole Hotel. Original postcard.

Fransham School, now the
village hall. Photograph, the author.

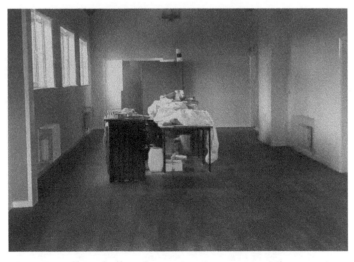

Interior village hall, redecoration in progress. The room at
the far end was where Spilsbury carried out the autopsy on
Rosaline Fox. Photograph, the author.

Sir John and Lady Constance Leslie. Image courtesy of Public Record Office of Northern Ireland.

The man who became Norris. Gerald Hamilton (striped blazer) with Archibald Walker, the 'plucked pigeon'. Image courtesy of City of Westminster Archives.

Manchester Square where Sidney was employed as a page boy by the Leslies. Original postcard.

Colonel Percy Holland, an
accomplished amateur actor,
was cashiered through
knowing Sidney. Image
courtesy of P. Duckers
thekingscandlesticks.com

Lord Lathom, playwright
and theatregoer,
'one of the finest and
kindest of men'.

Cavendish Mansions today, where Rosaline
and Sidney lived for six years. Photograph, the author.

Cox's Bank, or the 'Army Bank'. This cartoon from 1917 in *The Bystander* speaks for itself.

Grindlay's bank where Sidney carried out his forgeries. The railings still bear the name. Photograph, Andrew Fletcher.

Earl Beauchamp, Former
Governor of New South
Wales, and Warden
of the Cinque Ports in
ceremonial attire. His parties
at Walmer Castle were
notorious. Photograph, the
author's private collection.

Lord Glentanar 'offered
Sidney a job as his personal
secretary'. Like Lord Lathom
and Percy Holland,
he too had a theatrical bent.

Lord Glentanar as Poo-Bah
in the Mikado in 1925
on his Scottish estate.
From an album in the
author's collection.

Sir William Jowitt, later as Lord Jowitt, waits at a bus stop on his way to the law courts.

Detective Inspector Walter Hambrook (right) with colleague.

Sir Bernard Spilsbury in his laboratory.

Atmospheric old photograph of the Metropole
Hotel circa 1910. Image Dover and Kent Archives.

Sidney, from a photograph released during his trial.

J.D. Cassels, Sidney's barrister.

Norman Thorne, chicken farmer. An earlier victim to 'Spilsburyism'.

Clarence Parade, Southsea, where Mrs Morse and the Foxes stayed in 1927. Original postcard.

Room 66 of the Metropole, after the fire, and presumably after the furniture was rescued from the dump. Image, The Trial of Sidney Fox. Notable British Trials.

A model of Room 66 used in court.
Worth comparing with the above.

Sidney's police mugshot. It wasn't a good hair day.

Sidney's waxwork in Madame Tussauds. Image courtesy of Margate Museum.

The crowd outside Maidstone Prison in Kent on the day of Sidney's execution. Photograph in the author's private collection.

From the stage play Sidney Fox's Crime. Sidney (Sebastian Calver) and J.D. Cassels (Mark Curry). Image PBGstudios.

From the stage play. Rosaline Fox (Amanda Bailey) and Sidney (Sebastian Calver) at Southsea. Image PBGstudios.

From the stage play. Sidney (Sebastian Calver) blames J.D.
Cassels for his guilty verdict. Image PBG studios.

From the stage play. Sidney and Rosaline Fox (Sebastian
Calver and Amanda Bailey) visit Cecil's grave in France.
Image PBG studios.

* * * * * *

CHAPTER THIRTEEN

EXIT MRS MORSE

Hilda Fleming was preparing for the departure of her guests at the end of January, the nice young man who had been an officer in the RFC, his sweet if rather doddery mother, and the Australian aunt to whom she would claim she never actually spoke. They were a colourful trio and had been exemplary tenants, or so she thought.

On 26 January, Charlotte and Sidney spent the night as Mr and Mrs Fox in Room 549 of the Strand Palace Hotel in London. The following night, they booked in to a different room, the night after that to yet another, on all three occasions as a married couple. This time Rosaline was not in the equation. It was the first time Sidney and Mrs Morse had stayed somewhere on their own away from Southsea and the continued presence of Sidney's mother.

It may have been that Charlotte, who knew that the tenancy of St Helen's Towers was coming to an end and who paid the bill on each occasion, was desperate to simply be on her own with him. The three days at the Strand have an air about them of firming up their relationship, needing to go away and talk, anywhere they could have privacy. We do not know what they talked about, but the likelihood is that she wanted some sort of commitment from him. She had made a will in his favour leaving everything she owned and appointed him the sole executor. She had conspired with him to defraud her father. What was she to get in return? Another merry-go-round of seaside guest houses with Rosaline Fox in tow? Couldn't the woman go to live with Sidney's brother? Had not Sidney done his share of looking after her?

On the afternoon before their third tryst at the Strand Palace, Sidney and Rosaline went to see William to discuss her staying there for a period when the St Helen's Towers tenancy ran out, but William had had enough of his mother at Christmas and refused to be encumbered with her. They came away, disappointed and angered.

That night 'Mr and Mrs Fox' enjoyed their last night, if enjoyed is the word. What could be more wonderful than if he came out to Australia with her and started a new life? But Sidney would never leave Rosaline. She was his pal, his original and faithful co-conspirator. Charlotte had now been keeping both of them for months, but there was never any doubt about who Sidney would choose. For his part, it was likely he was getting fed up with the situation, of keeping up the pretence that he could ever be anything other than a homosexual man who enjoyed the company of his own kind and the fun that London had to offer. What was he going to do in Australia, he might have asked? Become a sheep farmer?

When Hilda Fleming entered the flat to clean up after the departure of her guests, she got a shock. Part of the furnishings were a bureau and a writing desk in which she had locked up a quantity of jewellery and a tin box in which she possessed about four pounds worth of threepenny bits. The jewellery and money were gone along with a pile of books, gramophone records and other small articles. She immediately contacted the police, who discovered that Sidney had disposed of the jewellery with a pawnbroker and stored the rest in a Portsmouth warehouse. This paltry haul of goods, as usual, did Sidney no good whatsoever; he needed to make up a sum of ten pounds to pay some moneylenders. It resulted in him being charged yet again and sent to Winchester Gaol for fifteen months, his longest prison sentence yet.

Only a few weeks before, life had been good. He had stayed out of trouble, at least as far as the eyes of the police were concerned. He had money, a benefactor, a will in his favour. As he always ended up doing in life, by committing a stupid theft, he kicked the sandcastle to pieces. This time there wasn't a wall or turret left, and when the tide came in, there would be little to show it had ever been there.

Charlotte Morse wasn't waiting around fifteen months for him to come out and go straight back to his mother, so she broke off their friendship much to the relief of her sons. In modern parlance, she woke up and smelt the coffee.

It was only after Sidney's sentencing that George Morse now broke his silence about the escape of gas in his mother's bedroom. He told his brother Reginald who went straight to see Hilda Fleming, who informed him that she had warned Sidney about the gas tap when they first moved in. She strongly advised Reginald to go to the police. Whether Reginald did or not, it took another two years before young Detective Constable Geoffrey Clarke of the Portsmouth Constabulary went to see her on the instructions of Scotland Yard, when Sidney was facing a much more serious charge than theft.

Mrs Fleming was unable to make a statement as she had suffered a nervous breakdown and didn't expect to be well for another month. Theft and adultery were enough to cope with in her establishment, but attempted murder was another. There may have been a second factor. Her son Charles' marriage was breaking up like his father's before him. The war hero and flight sub-lieutenant had made a good marriage, but they were headed for divorce, and ironically it was over her son's misconduct in a London hotel room. It was all too much for Hilda Fleming to bear, and Constable Clark went away with little of the information he had hoped for. She never did make a written statement about the gassing incident. And so the mystery remained.

By that time, a penitent and shame-faced Australian lady, accompanied by her two boys, now practically young men, were on the high seas on the liner *Ascanius* on the way back to Australia, where the fascinating young man she had met in England would be named as co-respondent in yet more agonising divorce proceedings by Captain Morse.

Totally disgraced, she went to live in Cremorne, a suburb of Sydney, with an allowance of thirty pounds a month from her father. When she died, she left an estate worth just over one thousand pounds. Her furniture was described in an inventory as being very old, having been used by her for many years, and of little value. She was not the wealthy woman Rosaline and Sidney had imagined her to be. She never spoke about her time in England. She once bluntly told a reporter who arrived on her doorstep, 'You know all about it.' By that time, everyone did.

Before his arrest for the jewellery theft, Sidney called at the boarding house of Mrs Winifred Taylor of Glencoe, Neville Road, Portsmouth. He had first met her brother, a seaman in the torpedo branch of the Royal Navy, over a year before and had been introduced to her. He asked Mrs Taylor to accommodate Rosaline for a few days while he transacted business up in London. He also spun her a story about a house in Portsmouth they were taking which was not yet ready.

Sidney must have known that the game that had seemed so promising had come to an end. The only house he was heading for was the big house, and it was more than ready for Sidney.

Mrs Taylor observed that Rosaline possessed only a small leather attaché case when she moved in, containing a woollen vest, flannel soap and toothbrush. Her clothes were shabby, a black dress, a coat and a small fur. Apart from that, she seemed to have nothing else. Life was now a far cry from the jolly days of her friendship with Mrs Morse.

Winifred Taylor visited Sidney in prison while he was on remand and asked him what on earth she was now supposed to do, as Rosaline had no money and no means of support. Sidney said he had no money on him, and his mother could not get any money from the bank without his signature, and he did not have the cheque book. Sidney said Mrs Morse owed him one hundred pounds and advised Mrs Taylor to write to Mrs Morse to get it.

Mrs Taylor did. Charlotte Morse did not reply.

After three weeks, Mrs Taylor went back to see Sidney in prison and told him bluntly that if no money was forthcoming, she would be forced to take his mother to the workhouse. This was the ultimate shame for anyone at that period. The last time Rosaline had been in the workhouse was when she was pregnant with her third son Cecil. Now she was older and frailer in body and facing the same humiliation.

Sidney once again expressed his opinion that his brother William should step in and do something. Mrs Taylor went to the hospital and challenged William to no avail. The landlady was disgusted that the only one of Rosaline's sons now in a position to look after her refused point blank to take responsibility.

The increasingly charitable and accommodating Mrs Taylor was becoming even more concerned that Rosaline had not one change of clothes and was starting to smell. Sidney said that some clothes had been left at a hotel in Portsea they had stayed in for a night, Totterdell's in St George's Square, so she went there and retrieved a few underclothes and two dresses. The rest was being kept on instructions from the police as the Foxes had left without paying.

Eventually, Mrs Taylor contacted the guardians of the workhouse at St Mary's Hospital, Portsmouth, and Rosaline Fox was admitted on 20 February 1928 as an indigent person. No money was supplied for her maintenance except the ten shillings a week she received from the Ministry of Pensions. She would stay there for over a year.

For Rosaline, who needed almost straight away to be transferred to the workhouse infirmary, it was a year without her beloved Sidney by her side. William never once visited her, though his wife may well have done with Rosaline's only granddaughter.

Towards the end of his sentence, and in the company of a warder, Sidney was taken from Winchester to appear at the Portsmouth Bankruptcy Court. He had been unable to pay the costs after his motorcycle accident, and it was judged that his liabilities were now still £267 while his assets were nil.

Even in the sombre atmosphere of a bankruptcy hearing, Sidney could not resist weaving a world of fantasy around himself. He maintained he had been in the Royal Air Force and had been invalided out because of a flying accident. The lie immediately painted him as a war hero. The court had no authority or reason to probe into the truth of the statement, but he came unstuck when asked about his mother's finances. She had, he said, always paid his bills because of his extravagant living and that after his unsuccessful action for damages, she had settled a bill of £400. Questioned about Rosaline's means, he said he believed his mother had an income of between £1,500 and £2,000 a year, though he had not the slightest conception of where that money came from.

The response by the official receiver, Mr Williams, was indignant.

'Did she strike you as a lady who was entitled to live at the rate of £1,500 a year?'

'She used to spend a lot of money,' Sidney said. 'She paid my tailors' bills.'

The official receiver suggested that Rosaline Fox had no income at all.

'She always told me she had,' said Sidney.

'Where is she now?' Williams enquired.

'In the workhouse infirmary.'

The registrar, Mr Payne, piped up incredulously.

'And no one has removed her even though she has an income of £1,500 a year?'

The examination closed, and Sidney was returned to Winchester to see out the rest of his sentence. When he was released, he was the dutiful son and removed Rosaline from the workhouse, even though he was now broke, as was she. They had also lost the security of a home and had little prospect of finding another, except by their combined wits.

Sidney could have left his mother where she was at least cared for. She now shuffled as she walked and was even more prone to falls. She also looked about ten years older than her real age.

Sidney had no intention of giving up the city life which had drawn him like a magnet from that primitive, isolated Norfolk community. He had a gay life of his own to lead, in both senses of the word, and it is notable that he elected to saddle himself with a mother who now needed care on a daily basis.

It would later be implied that his motives were not as genuine as they appeared on the surface, that he had ulterior designs. Yet no one ever saw him treat his mother harshly or even become impatient with her. When they walked, she always took his arm. At the succession of boarding houses and hotels in which they stayed after their mutual incarcerations, he would care for her every comfort and be there at her beck and call. Sidney had a word for their relationship. He said they were pals.

They had long been pals in crime, these two rogues. It was said that Sidney still carried Mrs Morse's will around with him in the hope that one day they might profit from it, though she had revoked it as soon as she got back to Australia.

What did they talk about, this odd pair, over an evening glass of stout, at a hotel which Rosaline knew her son had no money to pay for and which they would be obliged to creep out of in the morning as a couple of criminals? Homeless, rootless, with few possessions between them other than the clothes they stood up in, they made a fist of trying to remain respectable wherever they went. The sweet, doddering lady and the well-spoken young man, who looked like a gentleman by her side, but whose one suit, if one should look closely enough, betrayed the fact he was not of the class he tried to portray and never had been.

Sidney had taken the place of a husband and a provider. The man by her side now, youthful, charming, and resourceful, would never leave her like her husband Billy Fox did, never disappear up the tracks and abandon her to her fate. After all, had he not come back for her and taken her out of that dreadful place, just as she had always been there for him? In the remarkable odyssey that followed, he was in many ways her perfect partner.

* * * * * *

CHAPTER FOURTEEN

INSURANCE, INSURANCE, INSURANCE

Mrs Beatrice Warren, who kept a boarding house close to Kings Cross station, thought Rosaline Fox a most peculiar woman. She and Sidney stayed with her three times, taking two single rooms, but she often saw them on other occasions in the Gray's Inn Road, a drab, wide featureless stretch of public houses and business properties off which ran small terraces of shabby, run-down guest houses frequently used by prostitutes and their clients. She was of the impression Mrs Fox had been drinking, though again this may well have been the symptoms of the disease from which she suffered. As a respectable landlady, she was at great pains to say that Rosaline took no alcoholic drinks while a guest in her establishment.

Sidney would go out during the day and return to his mother at tea-time. This was the pattern of all their visits. There seemed nothing remarkable about it, and Mrs Warren assumed that Sidney was transacting some business or other in town. Sidney was, for they had plenty of money each time to pay for their accommodation. During the day, Mrs Warren would look in on Rosaline to see if she needed anything. She found it very hard to make conversation with her and did not think she was very intelligent. When asked, Sidney told her it was because she had lost three sons during the war.

Alice Spiers ran a guest house next door to Beatrice Warren in Derby Street, and she, too, accommodated the Foxes. In Derby Street, no one cared too much if you had luggage or not. She had quite a number of guests who stayed there for a night's lodging. The routine was the same. After breakfast, Sidney left with business to attend to and returned for his mother later in the day. Mrs Spiers lent Rosaline a brush and comb to fix her hair. She found her very strange in her manner, almost dazed and stupefied. Like her neighbour Mrs Warren, she got the impression she had been drinking, but echoing Mrs Warren, she said that Rosaline consumed nothing intoxicating while in her house. On another night she had only one room available, so Sidney assisted his mother to bed before going off to spend the night with one of his friends. On the third occasion they stayed, Sidney returned saying he was taking her back to Southsea. Southsea would become just one of numerous places where, from now onwards, their fairy-tale castle called home awaited this nomadic pair along with their similarly non-existent luggage. They settled the bill, which was five shillings per person bed and breakfast.

In the spring, they took a train to Norwich, not only to pay a visit to old friends in Great Fransham but because Sidney wanted to renew a life insurance policy that his brother Reginald had taken out on the life of his mother back in 1913. It was for ten guineas. Sidney had kept up the premiums until being sent to Winchester Gaol the previous year, but now they had been allowed to lapse. He wanted to pay up the arrears. They stayed at 19 Cathedral Street, where Mr Henry Shepherd, the Norwich District Superintendent of the Wesleyan and General Insurance Company, visited Mrs Fox and said that arrears amounting to twelve shillings and sixpence should be paid up (62.5p), a new book issued, and that a medical examination was required. The arrears were duly settled, Rosaline had the examination and the policy was reinstated.

While at Cathedral Street, Rosaline made her own will, even though she had very little to leave. Miss Bacon, the proprietress of the boarding house, acted as one of the witnesses along with a neighbour. The content of the will was hardly surprising but remarkable for its tone. Apart from two small bequests of items to friends, one of whom was Emma Youngs at Tavistock Terrace, she left everything to Sidney, with the exception of one farthing. This she bequeathed to William, 'in the hope that he will never need his mother'. This last will and testament finally and cruelly set the seal on the long-running feud between Sidney and William. The next time Sidney saw his brother, it would be in a courtroom.

Nightly bed and breakfast accommodation, the occasional hotel, train travel, the paying up of arrears on a lapsed insurance policy—Sidney needed money, even allowing for the times they left in the morning without paying the bill, though that was much easier to do in large hotels than in St Pancras lodging houses where landladies kept more of a close eye on their guests. He was twenty-nine now and could no longer live by straightforward prostitution alone. Lupson and Campbell, doing well for themselves in business, were, as always, ready to help Sidney out. Alfred Lupson was luckier than most, for he got it back. He lent Sidney thirty shillings so he could go to Norwich, which Sidney returned to him by registered letter a few days later.

During this period of desperation, when only a few pounds and the wiles of her son were all that were keeping Rosaline from the workhouse, it was time to renew an old acquaintance.

Sidney had not forgotten Earl Beauchamp. It might have been better if he had. The earl had forgotten him, or if he hadn't, Sidney was only one of many young men assigned to past conquests and from whom he probably didn't expect to hear again. His decision to now tap the earl was to have far-reaching consequences. Beauchamp was coming to the end of his days as a Liberal peer, though he did not know it. His wife's brother, the arch-Tory Duke of Westminster, still seething with disgust at the goings-on at Walmer Castle, was determined to drag his sister away from that loathsome husband of hers and at the same time bring down the Liberal Party, which he hated with equal venom. He set private detectives on a trawl of present and previous servants in a bid to gather the evidence he needed, and he was successful. The man he called his 'bugger-in-law' could count his days.

Unaware of all this, Sidney first telephoned out of politeness or perhaps just to test the water. The cook answered. He remembered the name he had used at that time—when you were a compulsive liar, it helped if you had a good memory—and told her that he was Wilson Fox, a friend of the Beauchamp family and that he had lost his wallet. The cook was clearly well-primed in matters such as these and offered to give him a pound.

An hour later, Mr Wilson Fox was on the doorstep in a light suit and trilby hat, every inch the cheeky blackmailer in all but name. The cook had no need to check his identity or contact Earl Beauchamp, who was in Scotland. One imagines there was a fund for such eventualities. Cooks do not as a rule remain ignorant of the sexual shenanigans between their masters and their footmen and other young men. Anyone with even a passing knowledge of *Upstairs Downstairs* and the formidable Mrs Bridges would get the picture. When Wilson Fox asked if it would be possible to have another pound so he could get some dinner, the extra money was instantly forthcoming. The door was shut, and Sidney left a little bit wealthier, though it would be far from his last attempt to use the Beauchamp family to his advantage.

Sidney was not quite finished with Norwich. In May, he went to the local branch of the Eagle Star and British Dominions Insurance Company and handed in a filled-up proposal form. The name of the assured was Rosaline Fox. It covered one thousand pounds death benefit in case of accident and also a sum of fifty pounds in respect of luggage. The policy was issued for the seemingly arbitrary dates of 4 May to 4 June, a period of exactly a month.

While insurance companies were well aware of the potential for fraud or worse, there was nothing unusual in such short-term tourist and traveller personal accident policies. Indeed, twenty-four-hour policies were often issued, intended to cover persons injured or killed while on their journeys. The maximum amount of cover was two thousand pounds, and for this, the premium was as little as two shillings a day. Although the railways had been around for almost a century, accidents were frequent, and many people were terrified of making long trips by train without some form of insurance, rather like today on inter-continental flights. When booking train tickets, customers were often canvassed to take out such policies. Pickfords were the agents for many companies, they received commission, and as one assessor put it at the time, 'they are out to get all they can'.

Sidney claimed that his mother never liked to go on a train journey without accident insurance, but what was unusual were the questions he asked when he went back to the office a few days later. What exactly was meant by an 'accident'? The clerk, Stuart Dunford, recalled two of them distinctly. Sidney wanted to know, if his mother was drowned in a bath, would that be an accident within the meaning of the policy? Would it also be regarded as an accident if she was poisoned by food in a restaurant? Those questions he put at his mother's request.

Dunford evaded giving direct answers. The whole conversation may seem redolent of an episode in a Hitchcock thriller or an American pot-boiling *film noir,* but the example of the bath had a very English pedigree. In 1915, George Joseph Smith, known as the Brides in the Bath murderer, had been hanged after he killed three wives by drowning them in their bathtubs for their money and claiming they had suffered fits. Dunford may well have remembered the case, but he happily issued yet another accident policy to Sidney in the name of Rosaline Fox, this one for the period 12 June to 26 June.

And that would not be the only, nor the last, policy he would take out on her life.

On 13 June, the day after the second policy came into effect, Sidney and his mother travelled to Birmingham and stayed at the Midland Hotel. They booked into separate rooms as Mr H. Wilson Fox and Mrs Fox. During the evening, Mr Gerhill, the manager, was called upstairs to the sitting room where he found Rosaline lying in the fireplace in a dazed condition. With the aid of a housekeeper and chambermaid, he helped her to her bedroom. Sidney wasn't in the hotel at the time, but on his return told him it was a regular occurrence for his mother to have such turns.

In the morning they paid their bill, which amounted to twenty-five shillings, but as Rosaline was not well, Sidney asked if they could stay a second night. This the hotel let them do. In the morning they walked out without paying. Sidney phoned later in the day and asked for the bill to be sent to Cathedral Street, Norwich. It was duly sent and went unpaid. What business Sidney had in Birmingham, other than defrauding hotels, was a mystery, but no more mysterious than the trips they made to Leicester and Coventry after Sidney had visited the Royal Insurance Company in Lombard Street, London, and taken out another two thousand pounds accident policy (premium two shillings) to run from 26 June to 26 July. Sidney already had a policy for one thousand pounds in place for himself with the same company which he renewed from time to time.

They were well protected once more when Sidney, on 17 July, left his mother in a pleasure park in Coventry and went off in search of funds so they could get home to London. This incident was typical of the haphazard life they were now leading and is worth recounting in detail. Coventry was well off their beaten track, as was Leicester, from which Sidney said they had travelled by bus. He went to Coventry Cathedral and told the custodian that he had lost his wallet, now a familiar ploy, and that he and his elderly mother had no means of getting home. The custodian of the cathedral, William Elliot, advised him to go to the police station which was only two minutes' walk away and enquire after a Sergeant King who might be able to help.

A little later Sergeant King duly arrived and found Sidney and the cathedral custodian, along with his own station superintendent, in earnest discussion about how best to help the pair. Sidney said he was an old member of the YMCA and had been there for help but could not find the secretary. Sergeant King said he knew the secretary, who was a schoolteacher, and put Sidney on a tram to the school.

Meanwhile, Rosaline was sitting in the pleasure park, looking at the flowers and watching the children playing. In spite of the name, it was not a fairground but an open recreational space. Sidney returned from the school to the cathedral, said the secretary of the YMCA could not help him but that he had afterwards gone to the railway station where they had issued him with a pass for himself and his mother to travel from Coventry to Euston. As proof, he waved a typed sheet of paper at the officer to the effect that they would pay the fare later.

'Good, that has got you out of your trouble,' Sergeant King said, thinking it was an end to the matter.

'Yes, but I was thinking about Mother,' Sidney told him, 'she has not had a bite or a drink all day.'

Sidney said he was in the employ of the Norwich Royal Insurance Company and produced another document headed as such with Rosaline's name on the top, which Sergeant King later thought might have been just an insurance policy.

'I am on holiday with my mother. That is my mother,' Sidney pointed to the name, adding, 'if you could help me, I will surely pay you back as soon as I get home.'

Sergeant King asked him if they had no friends or relations to whom he could write, to which Sidney answered that he had a brother but didn't like to trouble him.

'Have you got any money at all?' asked Sergeant King.

Sidney went through his pockets and said he had a few shillings.

'Well, out of respect for your aged mother, I will lend you ten shillings,' said the Good Samaritan of a police sergeant. Sidney said he could probably manage with five shillings but took the ten. By this time, Rosaline had somehow found her way back from the pleasure park to the cathedral, where Sergeant King shook the hand of the shuffling little white-haired lady and told her how sorry he was for her misfortune. She looked worried and was trembling, and he couldn't understand her.

'She is suffering from the effects of a stroke which she had some time ago,' Sidney explained. This time he omitted to mention the three sons killed in the war.

'You take your mother and get her a good tea,' King told him and left.

He never heard from them again. He later wrote to the address Sidney gave him in Cathedral Street, Norwich, but as the manager of the Midland Hotel in Birmingham had found, the couple had long moved on.

This episode and those before it encapsulate the lives of Sidney Fox and his mother at this time. The insurance policies were, for the moment, a kind of lottery. What was the point in taking out travel accident policies if they did not travel?

At any point on their numerous journeys, Rosaline might meet with an accident and cut her head or break an arm or a leg, and they could come into hundreds of pounds. Rosaline's condition also increased the considerable odds that while travelling she would have a serious fall. That was a far cry from planning and faking an accident, like pushing her off a bus or a train, which would one day be suggested was in Sidney's mind all the time.

The truth was, as all the evidence shows, Sidney shunned violence. So far as is known, he never gambled. But he might have been prepared to do so with fate, keeping the insurance policies going, just in case—as Mr Micawber might have put it—something turned up.

* * * * * *

CHAPTER FIFTEEN

FINAL RESPECTS

By August 1929, Rosaline's health was in severe decline. She was having difficulties in balancing and was slowing up. There was little in the way of medication and treatment at that time for what was then and is a degenerative disorder of the central nervous system. It was one of a litany of diseases for which quack doctors, who advertised regularly in newspapers, promised results from the use of electric shocks, but other than careful management in a safe environment there was nothing to be done for it. A life of moving from place to place, a homeless and hopeless existence of staying in boarding house accommodation, was the worst of worlds. The only other option for Rosaline was to admit herself to the workhouse infirmary, where she had already spent a year. The only option for Sidney was to put her back in one. That does not allow for the fact that in an age without social security, the workhouse was the ultimate disgrace. Victorians had lived in mortal fear of these institutions, trembled at the very sight of their forbidding walls and the knowledge that, once inside, you had descended as far as you could go. For a couple who prided themselves on maintaining a veneer of respectability and liked to give the impression of wealth, the workhouse was the last place on earth to enter voluntarily.

Rosaline had two bad falls in a boarding house in Argyle Square, just off Oxford Street. The landlady, Jemima Hunt, found her very weak and tottering. She offered to make her a cup of tea, but Sidney said his mother would prefer a glass of stout, a suggestion with which she readily complied. Mrs Hunt thought she was entirely under her son's control. Her husband went out and bought her a bottle of Guinness. Then Sidney went out for the night and stayed away.

About twenty minutes after Sidney left, Mrs Hunt heard a thud and went upstairs to find Rosaline on the floor, clad only in her vest. She was unable to stand up on her own, so Mrs Hunt assisted her back into bed. The following morning she took her up some hot water and a little later heard another thud. This time she couldn't open the door as she had fallen right across it. She eventually managed to push it open and helped Rosaline back to bed. She seemed to have no strength in her body at all. When Sidney came back, he opened his mother's bag and appeared to pull out a bundle of one-pound notes which he used to pay the bill.

'Do you realise your mother is very ill?' Mrs Hunt asked him.

'Yes, but I have a nurse for her at home,' he said.

Home was Cathedral Street, Norwich.

Gertrude Platt's boarding house in Liverpool Street was a place Sidney knew well, for he had spent the night with various young gentlemen friends there. Sidney and Rosaline took rooms for a number of weeks up to the middle of September, during which time he had another travellers' accident policy in place, this time with the Cornhill Insurance Company. They seemed to Mrs Platt very affectionate. The devoted son would bring his mother a bottle of whisky on an evening, as well as cooked meals, fish and sandwiches. They would go away for weekends, Mrs Platt knew not where.

One of the places was Margate. There they stayed one night only with a Mrs Staines, where Sidney inconveniently found he had lost his wallet and couldn't pay the bill. The landlady referred him to his mother for payment, but Rosaline, of course, had nothing in her purse.

'Mother says I'm a very naughty boy and want a smack,' said Sidney.

Sidney wept like a child, and Mrs Staines comforted him and lent him ten shillings. He and Rosaline then left, and Sidney came back on his own that afternoon, leaving his mother at the railway station, saying they had fixed up with the railway, who had given them a pass right through to Norwich where they lived. Sidney was still emotional, telling her he had promised to take his mother to France to see the graves of her three sons killed in the war and hated to disappoint her. She once again felt sorry for him and gave him another five shillings to get some tea as they had eaten very little food. She found him gentlemanly and refined; in fact, just the qualities a good confidence trickster needed.

Sidney promised to send the money once they got back to Cathedral Street, Norwich, but, of course, nothing ever arrived from Norwich or anywhere else.

Even their extended family of cousins and aunts were not immune from the machinations of the pair. Sidney's aunt Beatrice Rose, a second cousin of his mother who lived in Barnesbury, north London, received a surprise visit from Sidney one day. Rosaline had lost her purse, and they had no money to get back to their house, which this time they said was in Lyndhurst, in the New Forest. If the pattern of their frauds was becoming threadbare, Beatrice said she always got the impression when she did see them together that they exuded wealth. She gave Sidney a one-pound note, and he left. She never saw either them or the money again.

As summer spread into autumn, Sidney took out at least a dozen one-day accident policies for his mother, as well as another policy with the Cornhill, which he extended three times. They set off for the coast, where they stayed at the Grand Hotel in Dover on three occasions, paying for the first two but leaving on the third without paying the bill. Between those stays in Dover, Sidney found enough money to take his mother across the channel so she could visit Cecil's grave in the British war cemetery at Duisans, something she had longed to do.

Sidney had gone to the War Graves Commission six years back but lost the information, so sent a telegram from Dover requesting the details as a matter of urgency. On 23 September, they set off by boat to Ostend in Belgium and based themselves there, travelling to Duisans by train and bus. They were well covered by the accident insurance policy recently issued by the Cornhill in London.

Rosaline had never been abroad, and neither had Sidney, and this was the trip of a lifetime for her. Duisans was a few miles west of Arras in the French region of Pas-de-Calais and was itself about ninety miles from Ostend. Neither of them spoke French. The cemetery was, as all Great War cemeteries are, a sobering experience.

The rows of stark gravestones brought home to Sidney and his mother the full horror of a war that Sidney had avoided. The so-called Arleux loop was part of an intricate system of German defences where the British attempted to push the enemy back to aid the French. It had been a successful operation but one that bore a very heavy cost. Cecil had been wounded in the intense battle and died of his injuries the following day. His regiment went on to fight the disastrous Third Battle of the Scarpe River, where hundreds more died for no gain at all.

Duisans wasn't the only war cemetery the pair visited while staying in Ostend. According to Sidney, they had a cousin who was buried at Ypres, and this necessitated another journey of over fifty miles. It must have been an arduous four days for a woman in Rosaline's condition. If Sidney had really been in earnest about claiming on an insurance policy, the period they spent in France and Belgium would have thrown up more than one ideal opportunity, but it passed, as far as we know, without incident. There is no evidence they cheated on their hotel bills in Ostend, but it would not be surprising. Neither would it have been out of character for Rosaline's son to indulge in a spot of sex tourism while abroad to fund their holiday. Ostend had long been influenced by the British at play, and was more liberal than stuffy old England.

A compulsive opportunist, Sidney was not even beyond cementing new friendships aboard the cross-channel ferry. On their return he met a fellow passenger from London who was coming back from business, Charles Jason Clements. Sidney extracted the phone number from the forty-year-old widower and three weeks later would ring him up and ask for a 'loan' of three pounds. This was quick work, even by Sidney's standards. How he managed to have a sexual encounter on the ferry was possibly aided by Clements having his own van aboard which he drove for his employers, Mawers Ltd, auctioneers and house furnishers of Chelsea. Clements obligingly sent the three pounds to the Royal Hotel in Folkestone and never got it back, nor did he ever hear from Sidney again. When the police later found his letter, as they must have done, he was obliged to make a statement, and the loan of three pounds to a man he had met casually on a ferry three weeks earlier did not come across as pure altruism. Sidney's ability to part complete strangers from their cash was more than just survival; it was fast becoming an art form. (1)

After five days at the Grand Hotel in Dover, they left without paying their bill. Money was short again, and Sidney needed to up his game if they were going to continue with their preferred lifestyle. There were to be no more cheap boarding houses in London from now on. From Dover, they went to the Royal Hotel in Folkestone, where they stayed for nine days, penniless, without luggage but not without a plan. They had only intended to stay for one night, but on arrival in Folkestone, Sidney witnessed an accident between a van and a motorcyclist and was asked by the police to remain in the town to give evidence in court.

This prompted a very reckless move on his part.

By chance, which seemed to favour Sidney, Walmer Castle was just up the road. It was a perfect opportunity to try his luck once more with Earl Beauchamp, and there is no doubt he considered that. It was only three months since he had called at the Beauchamp family home in Belgrave Square and had been bought off by the cook with a couple of pounds. The castle was a different proposition. But he had another clever idea.

On 8 October, Sidney gave his evidence, which was about the speed at which the motorcyclist had been going. It must have brought back painful memories of his own accident and subsequent bankruptcy proceedings, for the motorcyclist lost. Then, in the afternoon, he told Florence Wright, the receptionist at the hotel, that he had invited Earl Beauchamp's son and daughter to tea at the hotel as they were passing through Folkestone by car.

When they didn't arrive, she advised him he should take tea on his own as anything might happen to a car. These were, after all, the early days of motoring. He did so, then put through a call from the hotel to the castle without giving his name, making sure the receptionist was in earshot.

'May I speak to Lord Beauchamp?' he was heard to ask. The head housemaid, who was in charge of the castle, answered the phone and told Sidney that the earl was away and not expected at the castle. In fact, he had left a week before. Sidney looked worried and disappointed.

'Is Lord Elmley there, or do you know if he and Lady Lettice are motoring through Folkestone as I am expecting them to call on me and take tea?' Sidney persisted.

It is unthinkable that Earl Beauchamp would ever have invited a sexual partner like Sidney to meet his children. Viscount Elmley was the courtesy title of Earl Beauchamp's eldest son and heir. Like his father, the young man had gone into politics and represented the East Norfolk Division in Parliament. Lady Lettice Lygon was Beauchamp's eldest daughter, one of the bright young things of the period and a flapper who, along with her brother, frequently featured in the society columns of the newspapers.

In time it would be suggested there was more than a whiff of threat and blackmail about these mysterious invitations. The invitations were, however, non-existent. Not even Sidney would dare to write to immediate members of Earl Beauchamp's family in such an unsolicited way and invite them to tea.

The castle housekeeper told Sidney she knew nothing of the movements of the family.

The following morning Sidney rang the castle again without giving his name and asked if Lord Elmley had visited. Again he received the response that nothing was known of the movements of the Beauchamp family.

Later the assistant receptionist at the hotel took a call from someone who she thought for some reason was Sidney's father, saying that if Mr and Mrs Fox were still in residence at the hotel, he would like to come and have tea with them. Mr and Mrs Fox indeed were, but Sidney wasn't in the hotel at the time, so she put the call through to Rosaline in her room.

Rosaline found herself talking to her son.

The next day, the receptionist said she had only thought it was Mr Fox's father as their voices sounded alike. Sidney told her it could not have been, as his father, like his three brothers, was killed in the war. It must have been Earl Beauchamp, he said, as he was expecting a call from him and was sorry to have missed it.

Sidney's calls to Walmer Castle and the casual dropping of the names of Earl Beauchamp, Viscount Elmley and Lady Lettice served their purpose. It helped when you intended to walk out of a hotel without paying at the end of your stay and asked for the bill to be sent on if you had aristocratic connections. When the Foxes left, they owed over fifteen pounds.

October was turning out to be a month of omens. On the very same day that he was dropping the earl's name at Folkestone, there were developments on the other side of the world. Captain Morse officially filed a petition for the dissolution of his marriage to Charlotte Morse, citing Sidney as co-respondent, alleging adultery committed between November 1927 and January 1928 at St Helen's Towers, Southsea, and at the Strand Palace Hotel in London. Two days later, it was served on his wife.

Sidney would not even have known about it. He was uncontactable, and Charlotte Morse was now history.

History of another kind was about to be made. After a three-day stay at the County Hotel in Canterbury, running up a bill which Sidney had no intention of settling, he and Rosaline were spotted by a keen-eyed hotel porter at a bus stop about to go to Dover. He intercepted the pair and encouraged them to return to explain themselves to the manager. During a fractious interview, the police were mentioned more than once. Sidney found some money to pay part of the bill, but they escaped without paying the rest. After one night in an apartment in Dover, where they left owing ten shillings, mother and son finally arrived at the Hotel Metropole in Margate.

The date was Wednesday, 16 October. It would be the final stop on the line for Rosaline Fox.

* * * * * *

Chapter Note

1. Reported in the *Thanet Advertiser* 29 November 1929

CHAPTER SIXTEEN

MURDER AT THE METROPOLE, OR THE MYSTERY OF ROOM 66

The weather had turned bitterly cold when Sidney and Rosaline booked in to the Metropole for just one night.

They would stay for eight.

Sidney asked for two single rooms with a communicating door, but not ones overlooking the sea, as his mother felt the chill. Vera Hopper, the receptionist, gave them 68 and 70 on the first floor. Sidney passed her a small envelope to put in the safe. There were later suggestions that it contained Mrs Morse's will, but this was never substantiated. The envelope, like the brown paper parcel, was a common trick. Their luggage had been 'sent on' to their house in Lyndhurst.

John Arthur Glen, a hat manufacturer's agent from St Albans, was holidaying at the Metropole in Margate with his wife, Augusta, at the same time. That evening, the couple, who, like Rosaline, were in their sixties, were sitting in the drawing room, he with a copy of the *London Evening News*. As travellers do when they pass through hotel public spaces like ships in the night, they fell into conversation with the lady who had recently arrived with her son. She was sitting on her own, and Mr and Mrs Glen felt she would like the company. She mentioned they had lived in London, where her son worked for the Sun Insurance Company.

Lying to strangers came as naturally to Rosaline as it did to Sidney. Mention of London prompted Mr Glen to tell her of an article he had read in the newspaper in which the writer described his loneliness in the capital.

Rosaline agreed. She told them she was very lonely and wished that she had a daughter to look after her, as she had lost three sons in the war, but that her remaining son was very good to her. Sidney soon appeared, and joined in the conversation. He told the Glens about taking his mother to Belgium and France to visit the graves of his three brothers. Rosaline was not feeling too well and decided to go to bed. Sidney accompanied her.

The following morning, the chambermaid, Louise Bickmore, brought him an early morning coffee. Rosaline took no breakfast and did not get up until about 11.00am. Sidney said they were staying on for an extra night as there were friends in London he wished to see and asked her if she would keep an eye on his mother, a request with which she cheerfully complied.

Sidney took the train up to London and met his friends Campbell and Lupson. He met Gordon Campbell at Piccadilly, and they spent the evening together visiting various public houses before going back to Lupson's house at Powis Square about midnight. Sidney spent the night with Lupson.

Mr Harding, the hotel manager, was naturally suspicious of any guests who arrived and stayed for extended periods without any luggage and made sure the bill was sent in to Sidney and Rosaline each day.

Rosaline was not well on the Saturday, and they stayed over until the Sunday when Rosaline fell down and hurt her elbow. One wonders if Rosaline's ailments were not partly manufactured in order to extend their stay. Mr Harding came up to her room with Sidney and found her extremely cold. Neither of their connecting rooms had a gas fire, so Mr Harding suggested they change to 66 and 67, number 66 having a gas fire with a penny-in-the-slot meter. This would turn out to be quite an important point, as Mr Harding entertained no doubt it was he who suggested Rosaline move to a room which had a gas fire. Her previous one possessed a coal fire, and it was never explained why that could not have been made up.

Mr Harding also advised bringing in a doctor. Sidney would tell more than one employee of the hotel that Dr Cecil Austen, when he came to tend to his mother, was drunk. He thought there was nothing much wrong with her, prescribed her some chloroform in water, and—according to the story told by Sidney—stuck his fingers in his ears, wiggled his hands and said, 'You're all right, old lady. Bogey bogey!'

When he told the Glens, the hat man and his wife from St Albans, they were shocked at such over-familiar behaviour and hoped that she was all right.

While this seems a strange bedside manner, it was probably just an honest, if eccentric, attempt to cheer Rosaline up. Unfortunately for Sidney, almost everything he did and said after this point was to be given a sinister interpretation or construed as a lie. It did not help that when he went to the chemist to fetch the prescription, he passed a dud cheque and took over a pound in change. Neither could he resist telling Vera Hopper on his return that the chemist had 'broken down' the doctor's prescription as an overdose could be fatal.

The chemist would deny ever saying such a thing. As Sidney breathed, the web of guilt around him developed yet another strand.

On that same day, the chambermaid helped him and his mother to clean first her coat and then his suit with a bottle of petrol, brought into the hotel by Sidney for that specific purpose. Dry cleaning with petrol as a solvent was a dangerous and, at that time, an outmoded way of cleaning clothes, for it caused numerous fires and fatalities, and it is astonishing that Louise Bickmore should have aided them. Dry-cleaners used chlorinated solvents, but for those who could not afford dry-cleaners or bother to wait, petrol was an easy alternative.

The bottle, almost full, for they used only a small amount, remained in Sidney's room.

There was no need to put any sinister interpretation on what Sidney did next. On Monday morning, he told Miss Bickmore he was going up to London and would not be back that night. He gave her half a crown to look after his mother. That day he called on the Cornhill Insurance Company again and extended the insurance policy to expire at midnight on Wednesday, 23 October. This was the policy he had already extended twice, but on neither of these occasions had he stipulated it should expire at midnight. One of those extensions had been to noon on 9 October when they had been staying at Folkestone. Noon was the usual expiry time of an accident insurance policy taken out for travel purposes, though it was not unheard of to extend one to midnight.

The following day, Tuesday, he called at the offices of Pickford's, where he filled in a form with the Ocean Accident Guarantee Insurance Company for yet another policy in the name of Rosaline. This particular type of policy was one that was generally taken out for one day only. Sidney once again explained that his mother was very nervous and would not go on a train without being insured. He was no stranger to these one-day policies and had by now taken out about a dozen.

For two shillings, cover was therefore obtained against accident involving loss of life for compensation of £1,000. For the loss of an arm, it was £500. They were going back to Lyndhurst the next day, he said, and so Sidney asked that the policy should run for the whole of that day.

It was now the second policy in his possession which would expire at the stroke of midnight on 23 October.

He had not enough money to get back to Margate, which should surprise nobody, in spite of borrowing a pound from Gordon Campbell. This led to another very complex Sidney ruse. He phoned up his old Kings Cross landlady, Gertrude Platt, to whom he had sent a postcard from France. She wasn't there, but he left a message, purporting to come from somebody else to the effect that if he, Sidney, happened to turn up, she was to tell him his mother was ill and to return home immediately.

Sidney just happened to turn up, and she gave him the message. Sidney said when he left her that morning, she had been quite well, but unfortunately he didn't have enough money to get home. Mrs Platt previously understood home to be Norwich and must have been confused to learn that it was now Margate.

She would have been even more confused to learn that the good folks at Margate believed the Foxes lived at Lyndhurst. No matter, could she lend him the train fare? She asked him for some kind of security, and he presented her with an old watch. No fool, Mrs Platt told him to explain it to the railway company.

Somehow after this dizzying and convoluted routine, Sidney found his way back to Margate and was just stepping off the tram from the station when he met Louise Bickmore about to board. The chambermaid was going off duty and said his mother had been concerned about him. Sidney went straight to the hotel where Rosaline was saying goodbye to the Glens, who had been very companionable and concerned about her, but were returning to St Albans. Rosaline said she was feeling much better and was looking forward to going home also, to Lyndhurst. As hotel crooks with no onward address, both Rosaline and Sidney were aware of the need to keep their stories aligned.

When questioned by the police, the Glens would be asked if Rosaline had told them of a premonition she experienced of looking in the mirror and seeing two dead bodies on her bed. They said if she had, they would certainly have remembered such a thing.

That evening, Miss Hopper presented him with his final bill, which amounted to £10.11.8d, but it went unpaid as Rosaline again felt unwell, and they put off their journey to Lyndhurst until the Thursday. Sidney said he had left his car in Canterbury, and they were therefore going by train. No car existed, of course, but as so often happened on their travels, a Good Samaritan came to the rescue. Miss Hopper was concerned that his mother might feel the cold on the journey and offered to lend her a fur coat.

The day dawned as cold as the previous ones during their stay. The chill came in off the sea and settled around the town. Muffled up against it, townsfolk and visitors came and departed, oblivious to the strange couple in connecting rooms 66 and 67. Most people with even the remotest interest in the financial markets were too aware of major developments on the New York Stock Exchange. Roger Babson, an American economist and business theorist, had warned a number of times over the year that a crash was coming and that when it came it would be 'terrific'. The day before had seen rapidly increasing volatility after weeks of frantic trading. By the end of that Wednesday, over two and a half million shares would be traded, and investors forced to sell at whatever price they could get. There would be panic until, six days later, the market would see its worst day in history.

It is doubtful that Sidney and Rosaline were concerned. They had nothing to lose. But little Margate had its own impending drama.

Louise Bickmore took them up early morning tea at 7.00am and found that the connecting door to Sidney's room was bolted from Rosaline's side. She was certain this was the only time during their stay she had known it to be so. This suspicious circumstance was offset by the fact that the night before when Sidney was in London, the chambermaid said she had found a chest of drawers pushed up against the door on Rosaline's side. Why this should be so is a complete mystery, apart from the simple fact that Rosaline would not have had the strength to push it there herself.

Of all the servants at the Metropole, Louis Bickmore had the most to say. She often saw Rosaline's clothes left untidily in front of the fire, strewn carelessly across the armchair, and her combinations on a cane chair in the room. By virtue of her job, she was able to account for all of Rosaline's garments, two stockinette dresses, combinations, corsets, vests, two pairs of stockings, one pair of shoes, a hat, a coat and a fur. On the morning the door was bolted, she picked up Rosaline's false teeth from the floor where she had dropped them in the night, rinsed them, and gave them back to her. The keen-eyed chambermaid observed they were held together by a spring.

Louise said that Sidney took his mother down to lunch on that Wednesday. The waitress, however, said they did not take lunch that day at all. About dinner, there was no conflict.

After a trip to Dover in the afternoon, Sidney and Rosaline came down to the dining room at 7.30pm, where Rosaline had a mixed grill. She enjoyed a half of bitter, and Sidney drank the same. According to Sidney, they spent a quarter of an hour in the drawing room before he took her back upstairs to her room. Much later, recalling the night for a piece in a local newspaper, an employee 'remembered' there was a band playing, Albert Crouch and his orchestra. Crouch was a local man, and his band appeared at many places along the south coast, but neither Sidney nor any of the witnesses made any mention of Mr Crouch being there that night. Sidney was even reported to have bought the musicians drinks all round, an unlikely event unless he put it on the bill. More than likely, it was a colourful addition.

It was now about 9.00pm. Sidney had two accident insurance policies in his pocket which expired at midnight. There were three hours left on the clock.

The legendary Alfred Hitchcock two years earlier made his first successful film, *The Lodger: A story of the London Fog*, a dramatic and, by today's standards, heavily stylised story about a woman who fears her husband is a Jack the Ripper-type serial killer. Only that year, he had finished making *Blackmail*, his first talkie, containing a memorable sequence in which a young boy steps onto a bus on which there is a bomb. Audiences sat gripped as the master film maker played with their levels of anticipation. If Hitchcock had been sitting in the drawing room of the Metropole Hotel in Margate that night, a place one feels he might have felt instinctively at home, he would have seen a handsome, well-dressed young man go upstairs with his shuffling, elderly mother, her arm on his, a couple who might be seen in any seaside hotel on any night of the year. It was in the commonplace, in ordinary surroundings like these, domestic homes, London omnibuses, hotel lobbies, that the unusual and frightening often occurred, and suddenly, without warning.

Sidney said he lit the gas fire in his mother's bedroom. She sat in front of it and asked for an evening paper. Sidney suggested she might like a glass of port and went to the Hoy Hotel on the Marine Parade, where it was cheaper, and bought a half bottle. It was poured and bottled from bulk and cost only three shillings, cheap even by Margate's standards, as the landlord would testify. Sidney would say he often bought Rosaline a half-bottle of port. She had about a quarter of it. Sidney drank the remainder. He also supplied her with an evening paper.

Sidney placed a cane chair next to her in front of the fire to act as a table. On it, as well as the paper, she also had some grapes. Before leaving the room, he took her dress off for her, something he usually did. He removed the eiderdown from her bed and wrapped it around her shoulders. That was how he left her, not forgetting the goodnight kiss. As he went out of the door, he asked if he should come in again and turn the light off, but Rosaline said, 'No, it is quite all right. I shall be getting into bed very shortly and I'll turn it off myself.'

It was just after 10.00pm.

The grapes. The newspaper. The dress. The eiderdown. The now empty bottle of port. The gentle throbbing of the gas fire in a slowly warming room. There is only Sidney's account of how he left her to go down to the hotel bar for a last drink. No other.

Downstairs, Sidney ordered a small glass of beer and read a newspaper. There were two bars, and he moved to the other for a second drink. He had a brief conversation with the barmaid Elizabeth Wager. He said his mother was feeling much better and that they had enjoyed a 'sham fight,' which was something they did when she was feeling well. This injudicious comment would later be interpreted as something akin to a boxing match. The damage done by that careless yet innocent remark would be considerable.

He was seen going back upstairs at 10.30pm by Mr Harding, the hotel manager. The hall porter would put it at 10.40pm. Sidney himself put it at the latter time. From that moment on, no one saw him until just before midnight. He went to bed in his connecting room and turned out the light. The next day, they were going to get up early and continue their journey. He went to sleep. He woke up to hear the wind blowing and his window rattling. He opened it and thought the smoke he could smell was coming from the chimney of the Ship Hotel opposite. He then went out into the corridor but could not see anything. Then, in his own words, which have a peculiar unreality about them, he suddenly remembered he had left his mother sitting by the fire and wondered whether she had turned the gas off or whether something was scorching. He opened the communicating door and was met by an impenetrable wall of smoke.

It was quarter to midnight on Wednesday, 23 October 1929.

* * * * * *

CHAPTER SEVENTEEN

'VERY MUDDY WATER HERE IN MARGATE'

Mr Sidney Martin, Trinity House and Channel Pilot for the Gravesend District, had just returned from conducting a ship to sea and was staying in Margate, where he proceeded to the Metropole Hotel with two colleagues. On entering the hotel, he remarked on the peculiar smell.

'I expect it's an old anthracite stove,' he said.

They went into the lounge to have supper, and a man came running down the stairs in a singlet and with a towel round his waist.

'What's the matter with that man?' Martin asked.

'Oh, he's gone scatty,' suggested a companion.

Then everyone started running up the stairs and, shortly afterwards, the body of Rosaline Fox was carried down. The commercial travellers, who had been playing pool and drinking beer just a few minutes before, had put out the fire and become the heroes of the midnight hour. A few moments later, the 'scatty man' staggered down the stairs in a dazed condition, according to the Trinity House pilot. He half-fell to the floor at the foot of the stairs, and Martin propped him up against his knees. Someone brought brandy, and after drinking it, the young man started to come round.

When a death takes place in dramatic circumstances, everyone remembers it differently. As he was running downstairs, a guest heard him shout, 'My mummy, my mummy!' Sidney's response when this crept into later proceedings was that he was not a baby. A story would also emerge that Mrs Harding, the hotel manager's wife, when comforting Sidney over the death of his mother, smelt smoke in his hair. She thought it odd as he said he had never gone into her room during the fire.

No one that evening, or the next day, suspected that the death of Rosaline Fox was anything other than a tragic accident which had left a young man without his only parent. Her newspaper or a nightdress, or something, had caught fire and spread to the carpet and the chair. Mr Harry Hammond, Chief Officer of the Margate Fire Brigade and a member of the Institute of Fire Engineers with twenty-nine years' experience, assessed straight away that the fire had started beneath the armchair.

The doctor who first examined the body was Cecil Austen, the bogey-bogey doctor who, either drunk or sober, observed that there were no external marks or injury on her of any kind, though he admitted he didn't examine the whole body. She was not burned, neither were there any signs of asphyxia, such as the rosy glow one got from carbon monoxide poisoning. There was no sign of froth or blood-staining at the mouth. In the absence of any autopsy, he came to the conclusion she had woken up, found the room full of smoke, and fallen across the bed. It was his firm belief she died of shock and suffocation.

A second Margate physician, Dr Robert Nichol, arrived as Dr Austen was examining the body. Sidney was extremely agitated but took control of himself and later asked if he could possibly see his mother. Dr Nichol accompanied him to the room where she had been placed, and Sidney remained by her side for a few minutes, then came out again. Dr Nichol gave him an injection of morphia to relax him. He was not struck by anything particular in Rosaline's appearance. He, too, saw no injuries or rosy glow in her cheeks. He would say that she did not differ in appearance from 'the usual dead person', whatever that was. He described her as composed and pale but advised Sidney to contact a solicitor to watch his interests at the coroner's inquest, especially if insurance was involved. He would later claim he had no idea why he said that. Perhaps, like Rosaline, he had a premonition.

Sidney told Dr Nichol something which he need not have told him at all, about which a solicitor might have advised him to stay silent. He brought up the remarkable coincidence of the death of Walpurga, Lady Paget, Rosaline's acquaintance during her Red Cross days. Lady Paget had been found only ten days earlier in the library of her house in Newnham-on-Severn, Gloucestershire, enveloped in flames after a newspaper she was reading caught fire and then set alight to her clothes. Notwithstanding the fact Her Ladyship was probably sitting in front of a blazing hearth, not a penny-in-the-slot metered gas fire in a seaside hotel room, Sidney thought it worthwhile to mention. In doing so, he gave credence to the possibility he had tried to copy it, hardly his intention.

Lady Paget, he further offered, had only just written to Rosaline shortly before her own death. How Lady Paget might have sent a letter to an acquaintance of many years back who was wandering from hotel to hotel round the south-east of England with no luggage and no forwarding address is hard to imagine. Less hard is Sidney's need to embroider the lives of himself and his mother with impressive connections even though it served him no useful purpose whatsoever. Once again, he opened his mouth before thinking. Had he done otherwise, no one would have been any the wiser about a connection to Lady Paget.

As advised by Dr Nichol, Sidney that very day found himself a local Margate solicitor, Mr Walter Wilson, who took pity on him and advanced him money as he said he was penniless. Mr Wilson, like most people who lent Sidney money, would regret it, but in his professional capacity should have known better. While he was able and willing to help his new client temporarily from penury, he was unable to save Sidney from himself.

Sidney was true to form when asked to make a statement to Inspector William Palmer of the Margate Borough Police, one of the first policemen on the scene. Palmer witnessed him in a distressed state kneeling by the head of his mother. He informed Sidney it would be necessary for him to make a statement for the coroner. Even in such painful circumstances, with Rosaline's body barely cold, Sidney could not resist launching into a catalogue of unnecessary falsehoods when asked about his background.

He had been educated at Framlingham College in Norfolk, he said, and a boarder in East House. His father was the proprietor of Fox's Flour Mills in East

Dereham. He and Rosaline had formerly lived at 19 Cathedral Close (sic), Norwich, but she had bought a house at Lyndhurst called End View, to which their luggage had been sent on. These were facts the police could easily check, but perhaps Sidney thought they wouldn't bother.

The inventions just rolled on and on. Their house had been in the process of decoration while they were abroad. His mother was independent and of a good income. Only the day before he had been to her bank in Threadneedle Street, London, an institution called the Bank of England, and cashed a cheque for £25, of which he kept one pound and gave the rest to his mother with which to pay the hotel bill. That money had disappeared from her handbag during the fire. It was a convenient loss as there was no money to pay their bill. It will not come as any revelation that the police later ascertained the Bank of England in Threadneedle Street had never heard of Mrs Fox, and no one of that name had an account there.

The inquest was held the next day in the town hall by the Borough Coroner, Mr S. J. Wilson Price. Sidney gave evidence, which the *Isle of Thanet Advertiser* dutifully headed in its report with 'Pilgrimage to Battlefields', and described how a devoted son had taken his mother to see the grave of his father shortly before she died. This may have been misreporting. If not, it demonstrates that even at the coroner's inquest, Sidney couldn't stop lying. At least the absent father made a change from three dead brothers.

'How was your mother the night before, how was she feeling?' the coroner asked sympathetically.

'Much better,' said Sidney, repeating what he had told the barmaid. 'We had a sham fight, a kind of boxing match.'

'A boxing match?' the coroner exclaimed, as though he had not quite heard correctly.

'Just in fun,' said Sidney.

After the two doctors, the fire chief and the staff at the hotel had given evidence, the jury brought in a verdict of death by misadventure. It was over. That afternoon, Sidney called on an undertaker and asked him to handle the funeral. His mother had always expressed a wish to be buried at Great Fransham, where she grew up. He also took the insurance policies to his Margate solicitor and asked him to expedite them.

That night was his last at the Metropole. He told Vera Hopper he was going to the Royal Hotel in Norwich, where he would base himself until the funeral. He later sent her a present of a book as a token of his appreciation for the care she had shown to his mother. It was about George Henry Borrow, a Norfolk author who had been born in East Dereham and wrote *Romany Rye*. Borrow led a nomadic existence, travelling in many countries, and penned a famous account of living with the gypsies in Spain. Sidney perhaps felt a kind of affinity with the Victorian writer.

He said he now had no relatives left in the world and that he would probably go to Australia, where he had friends. His bill, of course, went unpaid, and no one thought to press for it in the circumstances.

The next day he met Gordon Campbell in town outside Campbell's place of business and went to Dunn and Co. of Piccadilly so that Sidney could buy a new black bowler hat for the funeral. Campbell couldn't remember if he paid for it, but he left his old one behind. He also bought a suit, which Campbell paid for. Then they went to a bar near the Hippodrome in Leicester Square, which was the heart of gay London, and from there embarked on a pub crawl.

Alfred Lupson joined them for a short while, but he had a show to go to. At about 11.00pm, they split up, and Campbell went to a Turkish bath. That night, Sidney slept at Lupson's flat again. He cried and was in a deeply unhappy state. It was less than forty-eight hours since he had lost his mother, and he didn't want to be on his own. The next day, all three had Sunday lunch together.

Meanwhile, Sidney's Margate solicitor contacted representatives of the insurance companies in London on his behalf. One of them, a fellow solicitor called William Charles Crocker, who represented all of the companies, took a trip to the seaside to assess the situation for himself. Mr Crocker would subsequently be lauded as the man who unmasked Sidney. He left the Metropole Hotel with firm instructions that Room 66 should be sealed pending further enquiries and went straight to the post office, where he sent a telegram back to his employers. It read simply,

'Very muddy water here in Margate.'

* * * * * *

CHAPTER EIGHTEEN

HAMBROOK OF THE YARD

Mrs Dorothy Rose Gray of Thorpe St Andrew, a village just outside Norwich, was surprised when Sidney walked in by the back door of the village store which she ran. She was his cousin, though not by blood. Her father was Billy Fox's brother, and like everyone in the family she had heard nothing of him since the day he walked out on Rosaline and disappeared. She had last seen Sidney and Rosaline about six months previously when they called in for tea and said they were staying at Cathedral Street in Norwich.

'I suppose you know what's happened to poor old mother,' Sidney said.

She had only just read about the death in the *Eastern Daily Press*. She described him as very upset and crying like a girl. She sat him down, and Sidney asked if her father, his uncle, could attend the funeral in Great Fransham. Charles Fox worked at the nearby County Asylum, as did one of his sons, along with many people in the area, but he was almost seventy and in hospital.

He was not that ill apparently because he offered to come out the next day and drive Sidney and a few members of the family. Sidney arranged to meet his uncle outside the GPO (General Post Office) in Norwich, which was just opposite his hotel.

The following morning, in his new suit and black bowler hat, he went to the Norwich branch of the Cornhill Insurance Company himself, rather than leaving this one to his solicitor, and spoke to George Millbank, the manager. Not quite yet in the loop about the opaqueness or otherwise of the sea-water in Margate, Millbank was most sympathetic when Sidney told him that his mother had met her death in a fire. He asked about the origin of the fire, and Sidney explained that she had left some wearing apparel on a chair near the gas fire. Some of this had become scorched, caught fire, set the chair alight, and the fumes had suffocated her. He enquired whether, in such circumstances, there might be a claim under the insurance policy he had with them. Millbank looked up the policy and expressed his opinion that the circumstances were rather peculiar, and as such he couldn't yet say. Sidney volunteered that he himself had some doubt, a classic case of trying to avert suspicion by being the first to question it.

The next day his uncle Charles picked him up in Norwich and drove him, his cousin Dorothy and her mother to Great Fransham. There, in the small churchyard next to the school room, which held so many memories for Sidney, and in the presence of a small gathering of family and villagers, Rosaline was laid to rest next to her parents in a polished oak coffin with brass handles and a brass plaque bearing her name.

Mrs Gray would describe Sidney as sobbing and upset at the graveside. No headstone was placed on her grave. The sexton, Arthur Cross, who had been there all his life and remembered Rosaline as a girl, was present at the burial. He knew almost every secret there was to know in the village, including the truth about Sidney's real father, Thomas Newell, who was buried only a few yards away.

One family member who was not present was William. Sidney did not tell his brother about the death, and he only heard about it five days after the burial.

Back home in Thorpe St Andrew, Dorothy Gray asked Sidney if he would like to stay to supper, but Sidney said he really couldn't eat anything. He caught the last train back to Norwich and to his room at the Royal Hotel. What he did over the next few days is unknown, but he had plenty of time to reflect and plan for the future, one without the mother who had been by his side since birth.

A few days later, Mr Millbank called on Sidney at the Royal Hotel to discuss the insurance policy further. By this time, of course, Millbank had learned that the insured had met her death only minutes before the expiration of the policy, and in spite of the inquest jury's verdict of death by misadventure, he had grave misgivings. It was very muddy water indeed.

Sidney asked how soon the Cornhill paid out. Millbank said they normally paid out immediately liability was admitted.

'But in your case,' Millbank tactfully understated the case, 'there might be some delay because of probate.'

He asked Sidney what his profession was.

'I'm a farmer at Lyndhurst in Hampshire,' Sidney answered coolly.

'Who's looking after the farm for you?'

'I have a very capable steward who looks after the farm for me in my absence,' Sidney told him.

He was restless and seemed eager to get away.

'I have an appointment at Dereham,' he explained. 'I am going to see a lady about dogs.'

Millbank was curious and wished to know more. The gentleman farmer from Hampshire rose in his chair and picked up his new bowler hat.

'I am interested in becoming a dog breeder,' he said.

Had Sidney relied solely on insurance policies which covered whole months of travelling about the country instead of arranging with separate companies two which expired only minutes after Rosaline's death, he might really have been able to buy a farm in Hampshire and breed pedigree dogs into the bargain. A doctor had signed the death certificate, he and a colleague had observed no injuries, and Rosaline was under the ground. Unhappily, Sidney possessed no insurance against the journey he took the next day, Saturday, 2 November. Detective Inspector Herbert Ball of the Norwich City Police arrived and told him to pack his bag, not for a holiday, but to accompany him to the police station. Sidney had put an envelope in the Norwich hotel safe and retrieved it before departure. Inside, remarkably, was fifteen pounds in one-pound notes. This was one occasion on which it seemed he was apparently willing to pay the bill, which amounted to £1.4.7d.

Appearances were deceptive. The money had been advanced to him by Walter Wilson, his Margate solicitor.

He spent the night at Norwich police station, free of charge, then the following day was taken back to

Margate. Two days later, on 5 November, Chief Detective Inspector Walter Hambrook of Scotland Yard's murder squad visited Room 66 of the Metropole and officially took charge of the case. The room had been locked and sealed. He found the port bottle that Sidney had bought Rosaline that night, still with its wrapper, and the petrol. He had a gut feeling that this was going to be a major case. Hambrook was one of the 'Big Four' of Scotland Yard and 'Father of the Flying Squad' as he was described by the publisher of his future autobiography *Hambrook of the Yard, 38 Years of Manhunting*.

Hambrook's cases emerge from a post-war era when life seemed cheap and sordid, like the case of Ewen Anderson Stitchell or Eugene Le Vere, the more fanciful name he adopted, a one-legged tailor who sewed uniforms for the RAF and fell in love with a Camden cinema cashier called Polly Walker. Even the weapons he used to kill her were of their time, a silk stocking and a poker, found heavily blood-stained of course. Stitchell was executed at Pentonville.

Hambrook was to take pride in including Sidney in his memoirs. They had met before, he claimed, when he had been a young officer on the occasion of one of Sidney's previous arrests for cheque book fraud. Hambrook would pass down to posterity his opinion that Sidney was the 'devil incarnate' on account of his blue eyes, claiming that most murderers had blue eyes. He failed to describe the colour of Stitchell's.

It was not a good month for Sidney. While in custody, he was served with his copy of the petition by Captain Morse in Australia for dissolution of his marriage to Charlotte Morse, citing him as co-respondent and alleging adultery. This was somewhat surprising to Hambrook, who was also learning that the devil incarnate was homosexual. Hambrook probed into the affair and, from somewhere, heard the story of the gas escape in the flat at St Helen's Towers, Southsea. He immediately telephoned the Portsmouth police and asked if someone could pay a visit and take a statement from Mrs Fleming, the proprietress. Unfortunately, as we have seen, Mrs Fleming was too ill to give a signed statement, and it was left to a detective constable to jot down what she said.

Hambrook noticed immediately the connection between a gas fire in Southsea and a gas fire in Margate, though the first involved an escape of gas without a fire. Mrs Morse was back in Australia and had more pressing concerns than an unpleasant memory from her doomed romantic escapade in England, but it would not have been difficult for Hambrook to obtain statements from her and her sons. If he did, nothing is known of them. Hambrook well knew there was no evidence on which to charge Sidney on the Southsea episode anyway, even with statements, so he put all his energies into getting the Margate case together.

But what did he really have? The insurance policies were strong evidence of motive, probably the strongest he had ever come across in his career. As for opportunity, Sidney was in that hotel bedroom with his mother long enough to have killed her. But what about the means?

Therein lay the problem. If smoke was the murder weapon, did she just lie there and inhale it until she died? Hambrook possessed the death certificate, signed by Dr Austen. Shock and suffocation. What kind of shock? The shock of waking up and finding the room full of smoke, just as Mrs Morse had woken up and smelt gas? Sidney had rushed downstairs and called for help in putting out the fire. Was his mother already dead?

Hambrook knew there was only one way he was going to get at the truth. He had to exhume Rosaline Fox's body and subject it to an autopsy.

There was only one man for such a delicate and difficult job, and that was Sir Bernard Spilsbury.

* * * * * *

CHAPTER NINETEEN

PATHOLOGIST FOR THE PROSECUTION

A suspected murder, an exhumation in a quiet country churchyard, the presence of one of the big brains of Scotland Yard, and the most famous pathologist in the land made it national news.

The Hull Daily Mail, among other papers, fell over itself to describe the event.

'As dawn broke today across the Norfolk meadows, men with spades arrived at Great Fransham churchyard for the exhumation of the body of Mrs Rosaline Fox...a soft November sun shone down from behind the picturesque fourteenth century church tower upon the little graveyard...above it all, the wind sighed in accompaniment as it rustled the dying autumn leaves of the chestnut trees.'

Even the men with spades came in for their share.

'Presently there came the sagging sound of a spade as it sank into the turf, then the gentle noise of earth being thrown upon earth, and the deep breathing of men using their muscles and their strength.'

It was all lost on the villagers who merely glanced at the brown-coloured screen around the grave, including a shepherd who walked past with a flock of sheep and paid little attention. The pulley of the derrick protruding over the top of the screen moved, and there came the grinding of the rope as it wound round the wheel as the coffin emerged from its resting place. Present were Superintendent Mann of the Norfolk Police, who had come from East Dereham with a posse of constables, Mr Gore, the splendidly named undertaker from Margate, and Arthur Cross the sexton.

The coffin was raised from the grave and remained on the bier until the arrival of Hambrook. He had travelled by road with Sir Bernard Spilsbury, Honorary Pathologist to the Home Office, and his own 'big gun'. Spilsbury's reputation went before him. He was no ordinary expert witness. He had given evidence in many of the major murder trials of the era, and men had been hanged on the strength of his words and his opinions. For those who followed criminal trials, he was practically a celebrity, held in awe by policemen and lawyers alike. Public galleries were packed when he appeared, and juries, mesmerised by the great man, hung on his every word, relishing the forensic battles that inevitably ensued. Battles that Spilsbury almost without exception won.

Hambrook knew that if anyone could find the proof he wanted, Spilsbury could. In his memoirs, he captured the moment of their arrival like an excited schoolboy on a treasure hunt by posing one simple question,

'What would Spilsbury find?'

This question begged the assumption that Spilsbury would find *something*.

The newspapers reported they stopped for breakfast together in Cambridge on the way and if true, which sounds perfectly reasonable, they enjoyed plenty of time to talk about the case. Hambrook was aware that if Spilsbury found nothing but a slightly decomposed lady with soot in her lungs, no injuries to her body and no trace of poison or anything else in her stomach, then he didn't have a case at all. Spilsbury was conscious of his responsibilities. He rarely worked for the defence. He was overwhelmingly a pathologist for the prosecution, and his journey from London to deepest Norfolk, with a welcome stop for breakfast in the presence of the man in charge of the case, must be seen in that light.

Arthur Cross unlocked the door to the schoolhouse, in which a room had been specially prepared for Spilsbury to perform the autopsy. At a signal from the chief constable, the bier was drawn up to the side of the screen, and six policemen reverently lifted the coffin and placed it on top, covering it with a large tartan rug. Like a funeral in reverse, with heads bared, the slow procession to the schoolhouse began, led by Superintendent Mann. Inside the schoolhouse, which had not changed much if at all since the days that Sidney and his brothers had been educated there, Sir Bernard set about his task. As he preferred to work without any assistant, he would remain undisturbed.

There was no smell when the coffin lid was lifted, other than that of the sawdust with which it had been packed for the journey from Margate to Norfolk. The coffin had been sealed with putty, and the interior was still clean and dry. Rosaline's body was removed and placed on the table, and then the constables withdrew. Spilsbury would describe her as a short, stout woman, rather heavy. There had been only slight putrefactive external changes. There was much reddening of the back of the trunk, the lower part of the face and the shoulders, as there was of the arms and flanks, the expected post-mortem changes which occur hours after death when blood sinks to the lowest levels.

He inspected the body for external injuries but there were none. She had not been hit, or punched, or struck in any way that might have indicated the 'boxing match' which Sidney had described. The neck was clean and unbruised. He opened up the body and set about the task of removing organs and fluid to take back to his laboratory. Rosaline's heart was moderately enlarged and bore a patch of fibrosis associated with poor blood supply and disease of the arteries. Most importantly, the blood was thick and dark red and not the bright colour he would expect had she died of carbon monoxide poisoning. Knowing what he did about the case, he paid particular attention to the air passages and found those clear. They showed no visible traces of soot, the fine particles of carbon which would have been present if she had woken up in that room as the fire was burning and breathed her last. Whatever killed Rosaline, it hadn't been the smoke.

Spilsbury turned his attention to the larynx and the upper part of the gullet. At the back of the larynx, he encountered a large bruise about the size of a half crown, as he described it. He removed the whole organ to take back to his laboratory, along with portions of other organs, including the stomach.

It was destined to become one of the most famous bruises in criminal medical history, for the simple reason that once it left the old schoolhouse and travelled back to London in the possession of the most eminent pathologist in Britain, it would never be seen again.

* * *

Sidney, meanwhile, appeared at the Margate Police Court charged with fraud, the relatively minor offence of obtaining credit at the Metropole Hotel by not paying his bill, and the slightly more serious crime of running up debt while an undischarged bankrupt. It was the most Hambrook could do while waiting for Sir Bernard's report, which seemed to take forever. Sidney stood in the dock in a smart black overcoat, black tie and brown kid gloves, his hands behind his back, and offered no objection. He was sent to Maidstone Prison in Kent, the oldest penal institution in the country, from where he wrote to Alfred Lupson, telling him only that he had been arrested for incurring credit over ten pounds after being declared bankrupt. Lupson wasn't fooled. He could read the newspapers. Sidney asked him to do him the favour of sending the *Daily Telegraph* each day and also the *News of the World* on Sundays.

Lupson did not comply. He wanted nothing to do with it and had good reason. Sidney's arrest for murder heightened the danger for everyone who had ever slept or associated with 'the kid'. The police were already trawling through his known homosexual friends. Both he and Gordon Campbell would give statements that played down their individual relationships considerably.

They described going into pubs in the West End, but not which pubs, the times they had met and parted, but not what happened in between, the nights Sidney spent at their flats, but not who slept in which bed. The statements read as though their acquaintance with Sidney was casual in the extreme. Not even between the lines does one get a glimmer of any affection that either of them may have had for their friend.

Campbell was at great pains to dismiss a postcard which Sidney had sent from Brussels of a young lad urinating in a fountain, saying it must have been a joke. (1)

When the police started to make enquiries at the Royal Hotel in Folkestone, they learned about Sidney's tea invitations to members of Earl Beauchamp's family and his calls to Walmer Castle to ask if the earl had been there. This, in turn, led them to take statements from the staff at the Belgrave Square townhouse, where they discovered that Sidney had been paid off with two pounds.

Exactly what his relationship was with Earl Beauchamp was not difficult for Hambrook to guess, but the connection was enough to ring alarm bells. What other names could Sidney mention in court, if and when they ever got him there? The scandal that would engulf Earl Beauchamp was some months off, but enough people, including many within the police, knew of his reputation and his close friendship with King George. The monarch's son, young Prince George, was rumoured to have had a relationship with Noel Coward and had attended Beauchamp's parties.

Those in government with long memories would have been mindful of the famous case thirty years earlier at the Old Bailey when Lord Euston had challenged the evidence of male prostitute Jack Saul, who gave graphic descriptions of their sexual acts at the male brothel in Cleveland Street. That case touched royalty too, for

Queen Victoria's grandson Prince Eddie, heir presumptive to the throne, was reputed to be a visitor. The jury was then hastily reminded by the judge of the respectable status of the defendant in sharp contrast to the appearance of the young man in the dock, who had the effrontery to wear an elaborate ring and carry a silver-topped cane. Sidney was not beyond showing off either.

Nobody wanted a repeat of that unsavoury business.

While his officers gathered statements, not only from Sidney's male friends but from the landladies and proprietors of the establishments in which the pair had stayed, sometimes paying their bills, sometimes not, Hambrook grew more frustrated. What was taking Sir Bernard so long to write up his report? It was three weeks since their journey to Great Fransham. Sir Bernard was well known for the time he took, for his painstaking examinations, and was not a man who could be hurried. Hambrook just had to wait.

Finally, on 7 December, Spilsbury made his report. It was both remarkable and uncompromising. The cause of death was neither shock nor suffocation, as Dr Austen had stated, but strangulation. In spite of the fact there were no marks of bruising on her neck and throat, Spilsbury reached the opinion that Sidney had strangled his mother to death and then set fire to the carpet near the gas fire to make it look like an accident, in order to claim on the insurance. Hambrook could not have been more delighted. His man had not failed him. There was a lot to do before Sidney could be put in the dock, but Spilsbury's report was in the bank.

At 9.30am on Thursday, 9 January, Sidney arrived back in Margate from Maidstone Prison in the custody of two warders to be formally charged. At the police station, he met Inspector Palmer, accompanied by Hambrook and Sergeant Ayto of the CID. Inspector Palmer, to whom Sidney had given his first statement hours after his mother's death, a statement full of lies from start to finish, wondered if prison had brought him back to a state of reality. It hadn't.

Inspector Palmer asked him to confirm his name and address.

'Sidney Harry Fox, of End View, Lyndhurst, Hampshire,' Sidney said, sticking doggedly to the place where the gentleman farmer and canine breeder of his imagination still held sway. There was never any such address as End View, and the police knew it.

He was taken next door to one of the Margate council committee rooms, described as 'homely' by the newspapers. A fire was blazing in the hearth, while lining the walls were portraits of former mayors and local dignitaries. Anything less like a police court would be hard to imagine. An ancient clock ticked off the minutes as the magistrates, a dozen of them including one woman, filed solemnly into the room and took their places. There was a full quota of members of the public, and those who couldn't squeeze in waited outside the police station for a glimpse of the man who was about to be charged with the murder of his mother, a heinous, almost unparalleled crime and one that was hard to imagine. Sidney wore a tight-fitting overcoat, a dark suit with a blue collar and shirt and black tie, and was described as medium height, with a pale face in which were set two strikingly blue eyes, those same eyes that had confirmed in Hambrook's mind the impression that he was the devil himself.

After the usual formalities, Sidney was formally charged with his mother's murder. He was remanded for a week.

'It is absolutely untrue. I deny every word of it. I have nothing further to say until I have consulted my solicitor, Mr George Hindle, of London,' Sidney said.

Mr Hindle rose to his feet and confirmed that he was now acting on behalf of Sidney.

Newspapers often say that the prisoner betrayed no emotion. Sidney's case was no exception. Turning to the chairman of the bench, he made a dramatic exit. He performed a flourishing double bow, smiled broadly, turned to his right in a military manner, and followed by the warders, left the dock.

Sidney was not without support. In the past, his mother had been the whole edifice of his life. Now that prison was his only home, his allies would range from other senior pathologists to boarding house landladies and, perhaps surprisingly, a female crime writer. Many thousands of others across the country could scarcely believe that the handsome, fresh-faced boy, who just a few weeks before had taken his mother on a pilgrimage to see the grave of his brother, would set upon her in such a ghastly, premeditated way.

The police had other information. They knew about the frauds, the prison sentences, and the incident concerning Charlotte Morse. They possessed a list of his sexual partners. Worse, the fact he had gone to Earl Beauchamp's house in Belgrave Square asking for money and professed to know his children was, in their eyes, indicative of a dangerous man who could employ blackmail and probably had done so many times.

Eight days later, Sidney was returned to Margate from Maidstone Prison for the seven days of committal proceedings, where the evidence against him was aired in open court with no reporting restrictions and in full view of the public. These were held in the council chamber of the Town Hall, in which a large wooden dock on rubber wheels was brought in to accommodate him. It must have felt uncomfortably like the timbrel taking men to be hanged at Newgate.

It was reported in the *Portsmouth Evening News*, which never failed to mention that the accused and his mother had lived in Southsea, that the long queue to get in was composed almost entirely of women, and that those who couldn't gain admission joined a crowd of between two and three hundred who waited outside.

The case was opened by Mr Arthur Sefton-Cohen, the assistant prosecutor, formerly a captain in the Royal Army Service Corps. Sidney was defended by his new solicitor George Hindle. His need for fresh legal representation became apparent when Walter Wilson, the Margate solicitor, appeared on subpoena and was asked if he had made certain advances of money to his client. He declined to answer and claimed professional privilege. Sefton-Cohen said that as the insurance claims at the heart of the case were fraudulent, there could be no possibility of privilege. He had become part of the case.

'That places me in a very difficult position,' Wilson addressed the bench. 'It is a question of the honour of the profession.'

Reminded he was now in the position of an ordinary witness asked about an ordinary fact, Wilson admitted he had advanced Sidney sums of money totalling forty pounds. His kindness had backfired. George Hindle from Battersea was not such a soft touch. Years earlier, he and a colleague made news when they smashed down the door of a house in which his wife was living a double life with their Japanese lodger. He sued for divorce, the papers relishing the 'white woman in the Japanese man's arms' angle. George Hindle would prove a tough adversary.

The first of many days of hearings got off to a dramatic start when Sefton-Cohen, anticipating the evidence that Sidney had always been good to Rosaline, told the magistrates, 'You will be driven to the conclusion that this show of affection to his mother was either assumed to deceive or due to remorse.'

Clenching his fists, Sidney leant forward in tears and shouted, 'How dare you say such a thing!'

Sefton-Cohen spoke for just over an hour, outlining the case for a 'deliberately planned murder'. Then Vera Hopper, the receptionist at the Metropole, took the stand and produced the book and the letter that Sidney had written to her from Norwich.

Sefton-Cohen read the letter aloud, his cold legal tone brutal and cynical.

'I am sending a small book about Borrow, which I hope you will like. I am not feeling too well. It does not seem possible that last week the poor dear soul was well. How I shall miss her. We had been such pals. There is one thing I do thank God for, and that is the dear kind friends who did so much to help me.'

Sidney broke down at that point. On the second day, there was another rush for seats. The burnt armchair and carpet were brought into the chamber. Members of the public leant forward for a better look. Mr Harding, the hotel manager, revealed the source of the story that Rosaline Fox had experienced a premonition about her death. Sidney, he said, had recounted it himself after the inquest, when they were sitting back in the hotel with a drink. Sidney told him that the day before, his mother had been looking in the mirror and thought she saw two dead bodies on the bed. Sidney adjusted the bedclothes, and the bodies she imagined immediately disappeared.

On the third day of the proceedings, there was no imagining the lean, straight figure of Sir Bernard Spilsbury, who entered and took a seat at the solicitor's table. His evidence, which was the most eagerly awaited of the day, changed the whole outlook on the case.

Microscopic examination of the inner surfaces of the air passages revealed no trace of soot. Rosaline had not been alive when the smoke filled the room. There was no carbon monoxide in the blood. Not only had he found the half-crown size bruise on the back of the larynx, but there had been bruising on the left side of the thyroid gland, and on the tongue there was a third bruise the size of a pea. The injuries, he boldly stated, in spite of no external bruising whatsoever, could only be accounted for by manual strangulation by the hand or hands, causing death by asphyxia. When it was suggested to him that in cases of strangulation by the hand, it was surely more usual to find marks on the outer skin of the neck, Spilsbury had a ready answer that begged further questioning. *There might not be any if the victim offered very little resistance, and the fingers were pressed in the same position until death occurred.* He did not elucidate on why Rosaline should have slept quietly while being strangled to death.

George Hindle was cynical about the time it had taken Sir Bernard to reach such conclusions.

The exhumation had taken place sixteen days after the burial, on 9 November. Spilsbury had made his report on 7 December, almost a month later. Asked by Hindle if he could explain the delay, considering that a man might be charged with murder, he gave a very simple, unequivocal and unhelpful answer.

'No, sir.'

Sefton-Cohen came to the distinguished pathologist's defence.

'I'm afraid this is not one of the questions you can put to this witness,' he told Hindle.

Hindle was having none of it.

'I do not know, I maintain that it is. My point is a simple one. The report was made as long ago as 7 December. Why is it nearly a month afterwards that the charge of murder is preferred? Sir Bernard either knows or he does not know.'

Hindle was in fact wondering not only why it took Sir Bernard a month to make his report but why it was another month before his client was charged with murder. The Christmas break could hardly account for it.

'This is a matter of comment which the witness cannot possibly answer,' Sefton-Cohen persisted. 'It is a matter for the prosecution to answer.'

When Spilsbury went into final details about how he had removed the tongue for examination, Sidney lowered his head until his features were hidden by the dock. He did not want people to see him cry.

Dr Nichol's evidence which followed was more supportive of him. Nichol had been extremely sympathetic to Sidney, who had, according to him, been genuinely distressed by his mother's death.

Hindle raised an objection to Inspector Palmer recounting Sidney's catalogue of untruths as evidence of his intention to deceive. To anyone who studied them, they were the lies of a compulsive fantasist, not a man who was trying to cover his tracks. Sidney was even accused of lying when he said that Dr Austen was drunk on the day he attended his mother.

In fact, half of Margate already knew that Dr Austen was an alcoholic. So did the police. He appeared none too steady on his feet when he stood up to give evidence of why he had initially thought shock and suffocation were the causes of death. (2)

On the penultimate day of the committal proceedings, Harry Hammond, Chief Officer of the Margate Fire Brigade, described the tests he had done with Inspector Hambrook to try and replicate a fire of the type that had broken out in Room 66. These experiments involved using horsehair, cotton wool and newspaper, with petrol and without. There were nine inches of unburnt carpet between the gas fire and the seat of the blaze, and he tried to bridge it but couldn't. In all his tests, he found it impossible to burn the carpet, except for the pile.

The insurance policies were, of course, a devastating part of the evidence. No less so was what William Fox had to say when he came into court to demonstrate that blood ran considerably thinner than water in the Fox family. He was shown numerous signatures of his mother on cheques, proposal forms and letters and said that none of them were hers. His mother's signature was shaky, more of a scrawl, and spread all over the page. The jury, of course, knew nothing of Sidney's previous convictions for forgery. William had seen practically nothing of his mother in recent years. Neither was he a handwriting expert. Hindle stepped in to undo the damage. He cut a hole in a sheet of paper and put it over one of the exhibits so only the signature and not the rest of the document could be seen, and asked William if it was his mother's. William was flummoxed by the tactic and admitted it might have been his mother's 'from some time ago'. That damaged his evidence considerably, though his hostility to his brother was undiminished.

The committal proceedings ended, and Sidney was sent for trial. The assizes were about to start at the county town of Lewes in Sussex, where a police officer wryly commented to a well-known crime reporter, Leonard Knowles, 'We couldn't keep him waiting, could we?'

Spilsbury had kept everybody waiting a month, but Sidney was to be hustled through the system. Knowles would follow the trial avidly and describe the evidence as among the most unusual he had ever heard in a murder trial.

A freelance journalist and aspiring playwright, Adelaide Foster, who had also attended the committal, was likewise struck by the nature of the evidence. By a strange coincidence, she was preparing for the production of her first play, one that was inspired by yet another sensational case in which the evidence had been just as black.

Mrs Foster would follow this one closely, to the point where it wasn't just the case that obsessed her but Sidney as well.

* * * * * *

Chapter Notes

1. Gordon Campbell didn't entirely escape the law. They caught up with the silk goods salesman ten years later when he was arrested for persistently importuning men at Victoria station. He struggled with the constable and demanded he be let go, saying he and his friend were on their way to Brighton, had got drunk, and missed their train. He appeared at Westminster Police Court and was sent to prison for three months.

2. Dr Austen would appear in court himself three years later accused of possessing six rounds of ammunition without a certificate after his son accidentally shot another boy with his father's revolver. Dr Austen had 'completely forgotten about the ammunition' which he had kept from his wartime days in Mesopotamia. It was a thing he said that 'could happen to anyone'.

CHAPTER TWENTY

DARK FORCES

Freelance journalism was not a career followed by a lot of women in the twenties and thirties, particularly crime reporting. Adelaide Foster's first stage drama, *The Thirteenth Hour*, was written and ready to be performed. It was inspired —some said based—on the case of Philip Yale Drew, an American actor, who the previous year had been suspected of murdering a tobacconist at a shop in Reading.

Drew was touring at the time in a production of a play, unhelpfully titled *The Monster*, a thriller set in a haunted house which had enthralled audiences on both sides of the Atlantic. The evidence against him was purely circumstantial, as it was in Sidney's case, but it was devastating and provided a disturbingly perfect example of how an innocent person could become enmeshed in a web of evidence to the extent that his life might be put in jeopardy. Another seasoned crime reporter, Bernard O'Donnell, claimed to have helped produce the vital witness for Drew's defence at the eleventh hour, a fact that inspired the title of Adelaide Foster's play.

A number of factors make Adelaide's connection to the case intriguing. Drew never went on trial, but the inquest had been as good as one, turning the population of Reading against him. On his release from custody, the actor himself agreed to perform in Adelaide's new drama, which involved a suspected murderess subjected to a terrible third-degree ordeal by a detective. Drew was to play the detective, and the role of the suspected murderess was given to his new leading lady, a three-times married *femme fatale* called Norine Fournier Schofield who went by the stage name of Dolores.

A year earlier, a young artist who was in love with her killed himself by wrapping his head in an eiderdown, putting a rubber tube in his mouth, and turning on the gas. Dolores was now engaged to be married to her leading man, Philip Yale Drew, who presumably was of a less suicidal disposition than her previous lover. As Adelaide's play neared production, Dolores announced to the press with great fanfare that the drama had been written especially for her by Adelaide Foster. Adelaide had also been helped with her research by Bernard O'Donnell, who covered the Drew trial.

Sadly, the play never saw the light of a theatre. It was scheduled to open at the Opera House in Dudley and at the Theatre Royal in West Bromwich, but the backers pulled out and the money evaporated. The play had been rehearsed and scenery constructed, and an atmosphere of gloom pervaded the company until it was announced that the play would be produced at, of all the places in England, Reading. This was never going to happen. Many people in the town still believed in Drew's guilt, and the police were advised it could lead to a breach of the peace. The thirteenth hour came and went, and the drama with it.

So when Adelaide Foster heard about the Fox case, she was free to follow it and attend the committal and the trial. Besides, she needed a project to take her mind off the failed enterprise. She started writing to Sidney. The sensational aspects of it, matricide being such a rare crime, appealed to her journalistic mind.

Adelaide returned to her home in Tufnell Park in London, packed her possessions and headed down to Lewes for what was to become one of the most memorable weeks of her life.

Adelaide Foster was not the only woman to write to Sidney. He kept up a regular correspondence with Pridie Sinclair. She had always been fond of Sidney, and he of her, and she never forgot him. On his arrival in Maidstone Prison, she sent him a toy black cat for luck. Sidney wrote to her:

'I know how grieved you are to hear about dear mother. She was the dearest soul that ever lived, and had not an enemy in the world. I thank my God for every remembrance of her. How I have managed to keep up in spite of all these dreadful accusations I do not know, but I am confident that all will be made right. Thank God I have good friends who are helping me, so I must keep a brave heart. I have hung the black cat over my bed in my room. I must tell you that over here I have a family, one black cat that comes in at mealtimes and brings with it generally two others so I have a little company.'

A few days before the start of his trial, he appealed to Pridie to write to his counsel.

'Dear Pridie, there is something I want you to do for me. I did intend to write and ask you before, but it slipped my memory. Will you please write at once to Mr J.D. Cassels KC, the Assize Court, Lewes, Sussex, and tell him fully all about mother and myself and how I looked after her. You will know what to write better than I can tell you. This is my leading counsel. By the way, if you want to get the best report of my case I would advise you to get the *Daily Telegraph*. You get a better and more accurate account in this paper than in any other. My love, and mother's too; I know she would wish hers to be sent. I can't realise that I shall never see her again or see that dear welcome smile. I dare not think of it in my present troubles. It is just a little more than I can bear.'

Sidney was maybe not aware that James Dale Cassels had lost two previous murder cases in the same courtroom, those of Patrick Mahon and Norman Thorne. Mahon was an inveterate womaniser and soda fountain salesman who had dismembered his former lover in a bungalow on The Crumbles at Eastbourne. Thorne, a chicken farmer, had similarly dismembered a body, claiming that his girlfriend had hanged herself and that he merely cut her down and disposed of her corpse, burying it in his chicken coop. Both cases involved and relied on the evidence of Sir Bernard Spilsbury, whose damning testimony in the Thorne case might be said to be a precursor to the forensic duel that was to take place, with the same participants, during Sidney's trial.

There was another aspect to the choice of Cassels which should have concerned Sidney. He was said to have a particular dislike of homosexuality. In her introduction to the Fox trial in the *Notable British Trials* series, Tennyson Jesse, who met Cassels, said that Sidney had all but boasted of his sexuality to his barrister, claiming that he rarely slept with any woman except for money. It was typical of Sidney to open his mouth about such things. When he should have remained circumspect, such as the time he brought up the coincidence concerning the death of his mother and that of Lady Paget, he carried on damaging his chances one after the other.

Cassels was there to defend him on a murder charge, but the barrister's deeper prejudices remained, and it may well have been that Cassels believed him guilty. In 1930, a man who unashamedly slept with other men for money was capable of any horrors.

Because of the high-profile nature of the case, it was the new Attorney General himself, Sir William Jowitt, who led for the prosecution. The former Liberal MP had recently joined the ranks of the newly formed minority Labour government under Ramsay MacDonald as Member of Parliament for Preston and had been knighted on his new legal appointment. Therein lay another trap for Sidney, for Jowitt was a member of an establishment determined to keep the name of Earl Beauchamp out of the case, along with any other public figures, the names of whom Sidney might blurt out unexpectedly in the dock. Any evidence about his attempts to phone Walmer Castle while at Folkestone with his mother or his visit to the earl's town house in Belgravia was to be kept out of the trial.

Jowitt had handled many espionage cases and knew that Gerald Hamilton, because of his German associations, had been interned during the war as a possible spy, and that Sidney had enjoyed a brief relationship with the potential traitor. In his book *Some Were Spies*, Jowitt didn't hide his disgust that some were also homosexuals. He knew that Sidney had never abandoned his trade as a male prostitute and had carried it on right up to the time of his arrest. Sidney, who tried to see the best in everyone, even though only a few saw the best in him, went to trial probably unaware of the dark forces that were operating against him.

Sidney's trial opened on Wednesday, 12 March 1930. The Attorney General was assisted by Sir Henry Curtis Bennett, a fashionable silk of his day, who had prosecuted both Patrick Mahon and Norman Thorne but had also defended in some famous murder trials of the previous decade, including that of Edith Thompson in the notorious Thompson and Bywaters case. Probably the most amiable and kindly legal personage in court was the judge, Mr Justice Rowlatt. He was attentive, careful, hated being disagreeable, and took a scholarly interest in his cases, of which this was the biggest of his career. A total of seventy-five witnesses were to be called. Lady Jowitt, the wife of the Attorney General, was one of a number of fashionably dressed society ladies who were allowed to sit near the judge, a practice common at that time in sensational trials which promised great drama. This one wouldn't disappoint.

Sidney was brought from Maidstone in a saloon car with drawn blinds and entered the dock almost before anyone noticed. He wore an overcoat over his blue suit, and his hair was well-brushed. He kept the overcoat on as though he expected to be allowed to leave at any minute. The judge then told the jury of eleven men and one woman that they were as much prisoners as the man in the dock. His attempt at wry humour was outweighed by the fact that the twelve jury members would not be permitted to go home to families and friends until the end of the trial. They were given telegraph forms so that they could communicate with them.

Sir William Jowitt rose to make the opening speech for the prosecution. Their case was simple, that on 23 October, Sidney had strangled his mother in order that he might reap financial benefit by her death. She was in receipt of a pension of ten shillings a week; Sidney, he pointed out, was in receipt of eight shillings, which meant that when they walked into the Hotel Metropole in Margate, they had a joint weekly pension of less than one pound. In spite of their dire financial straits, they had stayed in other hotels and incurred debts they couldn't pay, with their only luggage a brown paper parcel. The jury settled into the picture very quickly. Sidney and Rosaline were hotel crooks.

Many of the allusions to his mother affected Sidney deeply. When the Attorney General referred to Rosaline as an 'old, frail and tottering woman', Sidney sat with his head buried in his hands.

Jowitt went on to build up the chain of circumstantial evidence, a chain in which they could not afford for there to be one weak link.

'What happened in Room 66?' he asked. 'What happened, happened in silence. There was no cry. There was no bell.'

Apart from Spilsbury's findings, there was also no physical evidence, but Jowitt went on undaunted. He would bring to their attention a pillow that had been placed, oddly, on the bedside table, in a position in which the chambermaid had never found it before.

'The accused,' said Jowitt, 'went up the stairs on the night of the 23rd, with a bill which he could not pay, with no money, with two policies due to expire in one hour and twenty minutes, which would entitle him to receive £3000 if the woman died by a violent death of this sort. He went up there with *murder in his heart.*'

Before the trial, Lady Jowitt had helped her husband and his prosecution team by obligingly playing the part of the victim while they, to a man, attempted to strangle her as she lay on a bed. They concluded, in the absence of any marks on Rosaline's neck, that her son had gripped it with his left hand, pushed upwards, and then used the pillow with his right hand to asphyxiate her.

'You can do it yourself,' Jowitt told the jury, grimly demonstrating on his own neck. 'Suppose a hand gripped and caught her throat, and went up like that…'

A number of the jury raised their hands to their throats. The Attorney General concluded with a question and attempted to answer it.

'What is the explanation of all the facts? I submit there is only one, and only one possible explanation. That explanation is that as Mrs Fox lay on her bed that night, depressed as she had been after half a bottle of port, sleeping perhaps—we shall never know—there entered from Room 67 by the communicating door her son; that he went to the bed, stretched out his hand, putting his hand upon her neck, and possibly, with the other hand, pressed the pillow down on her face, and so brought his mother's life to an end.'

Assuming that Rosaline was asleep, depressed by the port rather than enlivened, and not easily woken, the scenario contained all the melodrama of one of the silent German expressionist films of the period, conjuring the dark, silhouetted figure of Nosferatu the vampire stealthily approaching the bed of his victim.

Jowitt's only possible explanation was correct in just one detail. They would never know.

The jury, for the moment, were more interested in seeing the room itself, however. If they could not go home to their loved ones, they at least wanted a day trip to Margate to be in the room where it happened. Plans and photographs were one thing—a model of the room was also made—but how were they to get a real grasp of the feel, its size, its dimensions, and particularly the area around the fire and the bed without being there?

Mr Justice Rowlatt quashed that idea straight away, saying he had no jurisdiction outside of the county. Lewes was in Sussex, Margate was in Kent. Above all, justice had to be seen, and there was no way an entire court, a jury of twelve, the accused, and members of the public were going to cram into those connecting rooms. If the jury could not go to the room, then the room would have to come to the jury.

On the Sunday, the only day the court didn't sit, Room 66 was painstakingly assembled next door to the court. The jury had already listened to the evidence of the hotel guests who braved the thick smoke to drag Rosaline's body off the bed and downstairs into the lobby. Mr Hopkins made the damaging remark that her son had not helped in any way.

Dr Austen, who had signed off the death certificate with the cause as shock and suffocation, maintained he had seen no evidence of asphyxiation other than the fact the victim's face was slightly flushed. There followed an acrimonious exchange between Cassels, the judge and the witness as to the exact meaning of asphyxiation, which Dr Austen finally agreed meant deprivation of the lungs of oxygen.

Dr Nichol came next. He knew better. He coolly stepped into the witness box and cleared the matter up to the satisfaction of everyone with his knowledge of ancient Greek.

'Asphyxia means not breathing. It comes from the Greeks, where the word simply means no breath.'

He went on to describe the appearance of asphyxia.

'If a person had been garrotted or choked to death or by inhaling poisonous gas or being smothered, or killed by having a cord tied round the neck, or drowning…in such cases the face would be congested, probably swollen, the eyelids would be puffy, and the whole face would look as if the person had been strangled. The eyes usually look protruding and strained and the tongue is swollen.'

Mr Justice Rowlatt enquired if he had made a special study of it.

'No, but I have seen people gassed, half throttled and properly throttled,' answered Dr Nichol, supplying the court with an impression of the average caseload of a Margate doctor.

There was a hushed silence when William Fox took the stand. It was the fourth day of the trial, and one of the society ladies had placed a bunch of freshly gathered violets on the judge's desk. It was observed that not once did William and Sidney look at each other. William was described as an older man, sturdily built with square shoulders, in contrast to his slim, dark-haired brother in the dock. There not a vacant space in the courtroom when Jowitt read out the contents of

Rosaline's will, in which she left almost everything she owned, which wasn't much, to Sidney.

Then he came to the sentence that made people sit up.

'I leave to my son William one farthing in the hope he will never need his mother.'

William delivered his evidence in a straightforward manner, admitting that his mother rarely wrote to him and that he had not visited her once while she was in the workhouse infirmary in Portsmouth. He appeared callous and heartless, but he wasn't on trial, and the matter wasn't pressed. Had it been, it might have come out that Sidney didn't visit her either, for the simple reason he was in prison.

On the Monday morning, a shock was in store for the prosecution team, who had spent the previous day painstakingly assembling the items from the hotel room. The judge now decreed that the entire court could not be taken next door. It was impractical, for the same reason that he could not take the court to Margate.

The items had to be brought into the courtroom itself and there re-assembled. This took a considerable amount of time, care and effort. The burnt carpet, the horsehair armchair and the gas fire had to be laid out exactly as they had been in Room 66. Also included was the cane chair on which Sidney said he had put the grapes for his mother. This had a charred leg but had been found by the window, a suspicious circumstance if Sidney had later moved it. No evidence would be given that anyone else had, though in the chaos after the finding of Rosaline's body in the smoke-filled room, anything might have been moved. How it became charred would never be established.

Cassels, with the judge's permission, climbed onto a solicitor's table so that he could obtain an overview, and it was from that position he cross-examined Mr Harding, the hotel manager. Harding brought out the fact that in 68, the room in which Rosaline had felt cold, there was a coal fire, and that it was he who suggested moving them to communicating rooms with a gas fire.

If Sidney had planned to replicate the death of Lady Paget, whose newspaper had burst into flames and set fire to her clothes, it would have been the simplest thing in the world for him to ask that a coal fire be made up. Instead, they were moved to a different room which did not lend itself so well to such a scenario. Unfortunately for Sidney's case, very little was made of this. The prosecution themselves believed simply that Sidney had chosen to go the route of a fire rather than gassing his mother in case the similarity between her death and the near gassing of Mrs Morse at Southsea aroused suspicion.

Mrs Morse was not to be mentioned, in case it prejudiced the case, unless of course Sidney brought her up himself which, given Sidney's predilection for talking too freely, was quite likely.

Adelaide Foster, sitting in court, paid particular attention to the fire chief's evidence, for the enterprising young journalist would go home and try various experiments for herself. Hammond held to his assertion that the fire started beneath the chair. He had tried newspaper, a merino vest, horsehair and cotton wool mixed with horsehair, and saturated them with half a pint of petrol. His bonfire burned for seventeen minutes, and only ashes were left, the consequence of which was that the carpet had been burned through in only three or four places. His conclusion was that it was impossible to set fire to the carpet while it was flat on the floor, as carpets normally are.

Hammond also set fire to underclothes hanging over the cane chair with the charred leg and said that even if combinations had come in contact with the fender, the heat would not have been sufficient to light them. At the end of his examination, he said that he could not find any means of it being an accidental fire.

Cassels didn't score any points from a fire chief who, at the inquest, boasted that twenty-nine years' experience enabled him to assess the cause of a fire very rapidly and that he had come quickly to the conclusion that this one was accidental. It was widely believed that Hammond changed his evidence only in the light of Spilsbury's findings. It was an opportunity sorely missed.

Instead, Cassels asked that some experiments should be repeated inside the court.

'I suggest you take a handful of horsehair from the chair and burn it,' he said.

'I do not think that can be done, Mr Cassels,' said the judge, horrified. 'It may affect the air of the court.'

'I think it is important, my Lord,' Cassels urged him.

The judge consented. Hammond removed a handful of horsehair from the armchair and set it alight. It gave off such pungent smoke that the clerk of arraigns had to hold a handkerchief over his nose and mouth. For a long time, the court was filled with the smell. It is unclear what either side gained from this, apart from the knowledge that when set alight, horsehair burns.

There remained, regarding the fire, what Sherlock Holmes might have called The Mystery of the French Newspaper. This excited the court no end, because it was known that Sidney had taken his mother to Belgium and France. Inspector Palmer and Police Sergeant Herbert Fleet said they definitely saw pieces of what appeared to them to be a French newspaper. It was almost completely burned through.

Hammond said nothing about burnt fragments of a French newspaper being at the scene. Police Constable Bray, who had tried to revive Rosaline by giving her artificial respiration, had picked up only part of the *Evening Standard,* which had been close to the front of the armchair, but he did not say how charred it was.

'What sort of French newspaper was it?' Fleet was asked.

'It was a paper similar to the remains of the *Evening Standard*. There were French words printed on it. There were no illustrations, just words,' he answered.

'Is it in existence now?' Cassels asked, well aware it wasn't.

After the inquest, the stockings, handbag, corsets and pieces of charred paper had been put in a parcel and deposited on the refuse tip, where they remained for seventeen days.

'No, it has not been discovered. Pieces of the *Evening Standard* were all that could be found.'

They were in court, and Mr Justice Rowlatt himself closely examined them, turning the scorched pieces over with a paper knife.

It was revealed that over five hundred loads had later been placed on the dump, and when retrieved, the parcel was lying at a depth of three feet. It had become opened, and the newspaper fragments, with the exception of those pieces from the *Evening Standard,* were found to be missing along with a corset. (1)

Had there been a French newspaper, and had it been used to start the fire, it would have been a powerful piece of evidence if the date on it had coincided with the trip across the channel. They might well have brought it back as a souvenir, despite the fact neither of them could speak French. It seems incredible that, given suspicions were aroused pretty quickly after the inquest, the parcel was allowed to rot in a dump for two and a half weeks before being looked for, and even more odd that only pieces of the *Evening Standard* remained. One suspects that the French newspaper was thrown into the case as *un hareng rouge,* as the French say.

For Sidney, the most dangerous evidence still lay ahead. His own testimony, assuming Cassels put him in the witness box, and that of Sir Bernard Spilsbury.

Spilsbury's evidence, in spite of his exalted reputation, was still the weakest part of the case. If that fell, then the case fell with it. Everyone knew this. Privately, Jowitt had wrestled with the possibility that a jury, for once, might not give credence to the evidence of the great Sir Bernard. It was unlikely, but not impossible. In spite of all the experimenting with Lady Jowitt on a bed and members of the prosecution team gripping her neck, Lady Jowitt was still alive and sitting in court.

Could Sidney really have strangled his mother to death without leaving any external marking at all?

To appreciate how finely the stakes were balanced, one needs to go back a few days before the trial began to a laboratory in Gower Street, London, where four pathologists met to talk about a bruise.

* * * * * *

Chapter Note

1. According to the late Norman Dening, who worked for the company which had the decorating contract for the Metropole, he was given the job of re-decorating Room 66 immediately after the fire. He described it as being in a terrible state, a thick layer of soot covering everything, furniture, carpet, curtains and wallpaper. Everything had to be ditched, but instead of running it all up to the official dump, the Dust Destructor and furnace in Manston Road, which was a distance out of town, he and his men took it along the coast to Westbrook, where a new sea wall was being built. They tipped it behind the wall with the rest of the infill. This was, of course, before any crime was suspected. As Dening was preparing to re-paper, Inspector Palmer of the Borough police burst in and informed him that Sir Bernard Spilsbury was treating the case as murder and everything had to be preserved. Palmer 'nearly threw a fit'. Off went Dening and his men to where the infill had been squashed down with a steam roller. Everything was dug up, including the burnt armchair, and brought back. Had it been taken to the Dust Destructor, he said, it would have gone into the fire so he felt justified in his decision. This was related to local historian, the late Mick Twyman, and published by the Margate Historical Society. *'Murder at the Metropole, a new look at an old crime'*. The photograph of the room (centre pages) would suggest a freshly papered room with immaculately reconstructed furniture!

CHAPTER TWENTY-ONE

'IT WAS THERE, I SAW IT MYSELF'

On Saturday, 8 March, five days before the trial was due to begin, Sir Bernard Spilsbury welcomed to his laboratory three other respected pathologists. Professor Sydney Smith was the Regius Professor of Forensic Medicine at Edinburgh University, one of the most respected institutions in the country, home to the dark history of students who had cut their teeth on corpses delivered in sacks by bodysnatchers Burke and Hare. He had been Professor of Forensic Medicine at the University of Egypt, Principal Medico-Legal Expert to the government of that country, and had long experience of manual strangling. This was his first professional encounter with the great man. He would never forget it.

Dr Robert Bronte, for twenty-three years, had been the Crown Pathologist for all Ireland. He was no stranger to Spilsbury. They had crossed swords in the past, notably in the trial of Norman Thorne, the chicken farmer, in that very courtroom. The third man was

Dr Henry Weir, Pathologist to the National Hospital for Diseases of the Heart, the first of its kind. While Weir had been called for the prosecution, Smith and Bronte had been asked to appear for the defence.

When Smith published his autobiography thirty years later, the dust jacket boasted an image of himself intensely concentrated on dropping a substance into a test tube, while photographs and illustrations within suggested an impish figure, one in particular a cartoon of him wearing a kilt. The dust jacket was emblazoned with the question, 'Was he greater than Spilsbury?' Time would be the judge of that.

Smith was particularly intrigued to see the larynx, part of which Spilsbury had preserved. Spilsbury, he knew, regarded the half-crown bruise at the back of the larynx as the main prop of his strangulation theory. Smith examined it while Spilsbury stood behind him, saying nothing. Smith was not looking *at* the bruise but *for* it. He could see nothing. As he would write, he couldn't see so much as a sixpenny bruise, let alone a half-crown one.

'I can't see any sign of a bruise, Spilsbury,' Smith said at length.

'Nor can I,' said Bronte in his thick Irish brogue.

Spilsbury agreed with them.

'You can't see it now. But it was there when I exhumed the body.'

This quite staggered Smith because the larynx had been preserved in formalin ever since the exhumation, and if so, the bruise should still have been there. Bruising is caused when blood leaks into the tissues where it clots and causes the discolouration. After that, in death, it cannot go anywhere.

'Where's it gone?' asked Smith, perhaps tempted to ask if it had flown to the moon.

'It became obscure,' said Spilsbury, 'before I put it in the formalin. That is why I did not bother to take a section.'

All three visitors knew that a microscopic section of the larynx at the time would have been of inestimable value. Smith and Bronte were convinced that what Spilsbury must have seen was mere discolouration caused by ordinary post-mortem changes.

'I don't see how a bruise of that size could have just disappeared,' said Smith. 'A lot of blood would have to have been extruded.'

'It became obscure,' Spilsbury repeated. 'It was there. I saw it myself.'

'Spilsbury, I don't doubt that you saw something,' Smith told him. 'But I put it to you that it might not have been a bruise. It could have been a patch of discolouration from post-mortem staining or putrefaction.'

Bronte was nodding agreement with him as he spoke.

'We all know how difficult it is to diagnose a bruise with the naked eye after partial putrefaction has begun.'

Spilsbury politely refused to argue the point. Smith concluded his mind was made up, and nothing, not even the opinions of colleagues, was going to change it. He knew, of course, that Spilsbury had already given the bruise theory in evidence before the magistrates at the police court. Even if the eminent man had doubts, he was unable now to admit them. His belief in himself was so strong, Smith realised, that he could not conceive of the possibility of error either in what he had seen or his interpretation of it.

They turned to the bruise on the side of the tongue, which Smith said could have been caused by Rosaline

Fox biting her tongue with badly fitting dentures. The haemorrhage in the epiglottis was there, just a spot the size of a pinhead, which in his opinion could well be found on five out of six cases of death from natural causes. The alleged bruise on the thyroid gland, however, led to another major difference of opinion, this time between Spilsbury and all three of his visitors.

It was no more, in their opinion, than a few stray red blood corpuscles such as might be found in a section of any ordinary thyroid.

'I cannot accept that as a bruise,' Smith was emphatic.

Bronte and Weir agreed. Who would decide when pathologists disagreed? A jury of course. And as they weren't medical men, it was important they be given the fullest information possible in the fairest way.

The four of them discussed it for some time, and Smith, at the end of it, said he was inclined to believe that Spilsbury, even though he had not contributed very much, had accepted one small point. Regarding the thyroid, they were right and he was wrong.

But Bronte knew Spilsbury better. The Thorne trial was still fresh in his mind. There they had disagreed intensely over what were indications of hanging by a rope after the victim had been cut down from a beam, as Spilsbury maintained had occurred, and what were plain and simple neck creases. On that fine judgement, Thorne's life lay on a knife edge, just as Sidney's would do on what was a bruise or what was not a bruise.

'Not Spilsbury,' Bronte said to Smith as they left. 'You wait until we're in court.'

* * *

At the start of the fifth day of the trial, there was a moment of much-needed light relief when Dr Roche Lynch, the senior official analyst to the Home Office, gave evidence of the alcohol found in Rosaline's stomach. He'd found a small quantity of ethyl alcohol, such as was present in beer and wine, and possibly 'a few minims of port wine'. The volume of absolute alcohol would be about one drop.

'Would the effect of alcohol being carried through the body to the brain make one sleepy?' Mr Justice Rowlatt asked.

There was laughter in court. It was quickly suppressed.

Then Spilsbury stepped into the witness box and, in his measured, concise manner, established that Rosaline Fox's air passages were clear. She had not died of carbon monoxide poisoning and, therefore, neither the fire nor the smoke in the room had anything to do with her death. He had found signs of heart disease, but the amount was insufficient to account for sudden death by heart failure. Mr Justice Rowlatt helped to underline that point for him.

'That means that you do not think she could have died from heart failure pure and simple?'

'No, my Lord,' was Spilsbury's pure and simple reply.

He then held up a porcelain model of the human mouth, jaw, tongue and air passages, and indicated where he had found the bruise at the back of the larynx.

'In my opinion, it was caused by some mechanical violence, a breaking or tearing of small blood vessels. It was then that I had the first indication of the conclusions to which I finally came, that death was due to strangulation.'

He came to the tongue. The bruise, the size of a small pea, had been inflicted during life, or 'within a minute after the heart stopped beating'. He discounted the possibility that it could have been caused by the two constables, Bray and Fleet, putting their fingers in her mouth and pulling out and pressing down on her tongue to make sure there was no obstruction to breathing.

He said such a thing was inconceivable, 'even if she was alive'.

This was an astonishing answer for a pathologist of Spilsbury's reputation. To say that two constables manhandling a tongue during life to help the victim breathe could not result in a bruise the size of a pea was not only plainly wrong but totally absurd.

'When you find a bruise like that, how does it come about?' asked the Attorney General.

'Either by placing a hand on the throat and pushing upwards so that the jaws come together, or by placing a hand over the mouth to prevent crying out, which would also force the jaws together.'

'Is the bruise on the tongue in a position which would result from biting the tongue while having dinner?'

'No, it is not,' said Spilsbury. 'When eating, it is the tip of the tongue which is generally caught by the front teeth.'

'In other words,' Mr Justice Rowlatt once again helped him to make his point, 'you do not bite your tongue with your back teeth?'

'No, my Lord.'

Spilsbury said he had never seen such a bruise in a case of natural death. Regarding the small dark area on the thyroid gland, which he thought might be another bruise, he was willing to concede to his three colleagues who disagreed with him. For Spilsbury, this was gracious. But he wasn't finished with it.

Mindful of the experiments he had conducted with his good lady wife, who sat up on the judge's bench, and his fellow prosecutors, Jowitt asked, 'Suppose you had a case of strangulation by a pillow placed with one hand upon the face obstructing the mouth and nostrils, and the neck held in position as it were, would you get the symptoms you have found here?'

'It might well be so,' said Spilsbury.

The answer he wanted fell into Jowitt's lap. He sat down.

Cassels rose solemnly to his feet. Cross-examining Spilsbury was not a thing that barristers relished. At the start of the trial the *Daily Mirror* had published a short piece on Cassels, describing him as a powerful advocate and comparing his style to that of the great Sir Edward Marshall-Hall. Though one cannot now know the impression he gave in court, many of his questions fell short of that accolade.

'Is your opinion right outside the region of doubt?' he asked.

'It is, in my opinion.'

'Did you examine the mucous lining of the nose?'

'No because every person has a deposit of soot in the nose and therefore you cannot say whether a person died in a smoky atmosphere because of soot found in the nose.'

'Did you find disease of the coronary artery of the heart?'

He had, and in other arteries.

'Supposing Mrs Fox had dropped dead in the street, and in the post-mortem examination you had found these conditions, would you not have found sufficient to have caused sudden death?'

'No, not in my opinion.'

Spilsbury had an unequivocal answer to everything. He had built his reputation on it. He went on to maintain that the condition of her heart played no part in her death. Cassels scored a point when he asked how many bodies Spilsbury had exhumed in cases of death by manual strangulation.

'This is the only one,' replied Spilsbury.

And then Cassels threw away the advantage by resurrecting the thyroid gland. Spilsbury had already conceded his opinion to that of his professional colleagues, but now he snatched it back again.

'Is your opinion upon this part of the case (the thyroid gland) as definite as it is on other parts?'

'Yes,' said Spilsbury.

One can easily imagine Smith and Bronte sitting together in court, Bronte turning to Smith and saying, 'You see?'

On the bruise behind the larynx, Spilsbury became even more emphatic. To the suggestion it was putrefaction, he said it was a bruise and nothing else. There were no two opinions about it, in spite of the fact that there were, and in that very courtroom.

Cassels was on surer ground when it came to the bones in the neck. The hyoid bone, one of the bones in the larynx, becomes ossified and brittle in older people and is easily broken. It wasn't, yet Spilsbury had accidentally broken it in two places by leaning on it. He admitted it did not require a great deal of force. Neither was the cartilage in the neck broken. But Spilsbury brought up six previous similar cases in which only one resulted in the breaking of the hyoid bone.

'Have you propounded a theory that this woman was attacked while she was asleep?'

Cassel's question could almost have been worded to help the prosecution.

'I certainly think that is possible,' Spilsbury answered.

The cross-examination had a lapdog approach to it. Compared with those of the Attorney General, who was straining to get off the leash when Sidney went into the dock, Cassels' questions were often lacklustre and unexciting. Spilsbury was allowed to get away with murder, being definite on every point, even when common sense dictated otherwise. One of the final exchanges underlines this.

'Is it possible for you to have made a mistake and to have mistaken a post-mortem change for a bruise?'

'No, quite impossible.'

'Do you think the bruising of the tongue could possibly be accounted for by the tearing of the fibres of the tongue?'

'No, certainly not.'

'Even in life?' asked the judge.

'No, my Lord.'

A layman could have taken a sledgehammer to some of Spilsbury's answers. Cassels sat down. Normally the prosecution re-examine to undo the damage, but there was very little damage to undo. The best help came when Dr Weir followed Spilsbury into the witness box. In spite of being brought in by the Crown, he said that, in his opinion, there was indeed sufficient disease in the heart to account for death by natural causes.

Sidney had watched Spilsbury in the witness box for six hours. The man had been assured and impressive. Sidney was, in many ways, like a child who learned to emulate those who impressed him. Spilsbury was a gentleman, there was no mistaking that, with his positive answers, never once losing his temper and earning the respect of every observer in court. It may have been why Sidney, when it now came to his turn to enter the dock, put on such a calm and slightly arrogant exterior, instead of sounding less assured, which might have done him more favours.

Sidney would have an answer to everything too. One, in particular, would be remembered by everyone who heard it for a very long time afterwards.

* * * * * *

CHAPTER TWENTY-TWO

BRUISING ENCOUNTERS

From the start of his opening defence speech, Cassels was at pains to surmount the overwhelming evidence of the insurance policies and the impression they gave. It was a formidable task, particularly the timing of the policies that expired at midnight only minutes after Rosaline died.

'A great deal has been put before you about this "hour and twenty minutes before midnight", about the fire not being accidental, and a man going upstairs at twenty minutes to eleven intent on murder. Are you going to say that must have been the case, when the motive that has been put forward, the motive of insurance, had been in existence ever since the 4th day of May?'

This was the date he had taken out the Eagle Star and British Dominions policy and asked the clerk what constituted an accident. Between then and 23 October, there had been 176 days in which he could have killed his mother, including the period of the French trip, if that was his intention.

'Let those insurance policies have from you every consideration, but do not look at them from one point of view and say, "Oh, there was £1000 for death by accident" and ignore all the features of the policies…in my submission too much has been made of the insurance policies. The reason for taking out these policies was that, in the event of his mother meeting with an accident, they would provide a weekly maintenance which would have given her medical attention and comfort very different from that which she had during the thirteen months in the poor law institution.'

Cassels stopped short of sanctifying Sidney. He wasn't going to present his client as being a man who told the truth. They might as well know that straight away.

'I present him to you as a liar,' Cassels said, 'I present him to you as a man who does not tell the truth…he lied about his position financially, future and past. But, you are a long way, are you not, from finding proof of murder?'

This was the heart of the case. Not his lying. Not the defrauding of hotels. Not the insurance policies. But the proof that murder had actually been committed. Where was it?

He said he would call before them Professor Smith, whose experience in cases concerning crimes of violence was unparalleled and who would give a very different explanation for the mark on the larynx.

'What a remarkable piece of circumstance attaches to whatever this young man did, if murderer he be, if, in the course of the strangulation, he should have produced no marks whatsoever on the outside? You may build round a case of this kind a mountain of motive and surround it with suspicion, but if you do not prove that the person whose death you are investigating was murdered, your mountain of motive and your suspicion are without value.'

That point made, he put Sidney in the dock. He took Sidney through his life, carefully side-stepping the prison sentences, as well as Charlotte Morse. When he came to the night of the fire, he asked Sidney to tell them in his own words what effect it had on him.

'The smoke was very, very thick. The room appeared to be in darkness, but there was just a glimmer where the gas stove was. You could not get into the room at all. It knocked me out, made me choke.'

'What did you do?'

'I dashed downstairs as that was the quickest way to get help and raised the alarm for everyone else concerned because, obviously, there was a fire and I wanted help.'

There were dangers straight away for Sidney in this answer, and Cassels knew it. He must have known that his adversary was already sharpening his pencil. So Sidney had been more concerned about everyone else in the hotel rather than his mother?

'Can you remember what you did with the door when you rushed off?'

'I don't remember,' said Sidney.

'Did you ever grip your mother's throat upon the bed?'

'Never, sir.'

'Did you set fire to that room?'

'I certainly did not,' said Sidney.

'With regard to these sham fights, they were just playfulness, you were doing your best to cheer her up?'

'Yes, we often played together.' Sidney always sounded at his most truthful when he was talking about his relationship with his mother. 'It used to amuse her. I would sometimes hold her hands, she was rather strong in the arms, and I would purposely let her release herself.'

As he ended his examination of Sidney, Cassels may privately have wondered how many of those on the jury had strong, playful young sons.

Sir William Jowitt began his cross-examination. Sentiment left the court room.

'Do you always stick to the truth when on oath?' he asked.

'I do,' answered Sidney.

Jowitt read out the first sentence of his statement at the inquest.

'My name is Sidney Harry Fox. Until now I have lived at 19 Cathedral Close, Norwich, and I am now moving to End View, Lyndhurst, Hampshire. Is there one word of truth in that except your name is Sidney Harry Fox?'

Sidney corrected him. 'It is my name, but it should be 19 Cathedral Street. The Lyndhurst address is certainly untrue.'

Jowitt established that his expensive style of living, staying in grand hotels, coming down to dinner, cost vastly more than their joint income of eighteen shillings per week.

'You had no other income?'

'My mother had money from friends. She had gifts and loans from a friend, Mrs Morse.'

Ironically, Sidney fell into the trap by being too honest and too truthful. Jowitt seized on the name.

'Who is Mrs Morse?'

'She is a very well-to-do Australian lady. She was over here for three years and lived with us whilst at Southsea practically the whole time.'

'She was a married woman living apart from her husband, Captain Morse?'

'Yes, he had business abroad.'

'And Captain Morse has instituted divorce proceedings against his wife, and you have been cited as co-respondent.'

'Yes, I had the papers.'

'Had she made a will?'

Sidney said she had left 'certain moneys' to him. He admitted he had also insured her life in his position as an agent. It was at her request. That was as far as Jowitt could go on the Morse saga. Instead he brought up the similarity of the death of Lady Paget in front of a fire, suggesting Sidney had tried to copy it. Sidney said he had never met her. She was his mother's friend.

Coming to the fire and his big moment, he asked, 'Did you realise when you opened the communicating door that the atmosphere in the room was such as would probably suffocate anybody inside?'

'If I had stayed in there three or four moments I should have been suffocated,' Sidney answered.

'So that you must have been greatly apprehensive for your mother?'

'I was.'

Jowitt's next five words had a powerful effect.

'*Fox, you closed the door.*'

Instead of repeating that he couldn't remember, which he had told Cassels, Sidney gave a different answer.

'It is quite possible I did.'

'Can you explain to me why it is that you closed the door instead of flinging it wide open?'

'My explanation for that is that the smoke should not spread into the hotel.'

There were gasps of astonishment in the court at that remark.

'Why, at a moment when you believed that your mother was in that room, did you trouble one twopenny bit about the smoke getting into the hotel?'

Sidney tried to backtrack, but the damage was already done.

'I have not admitted that I shut the door. I very much doubt that I did.'

'Does it not strike you now as an inconceivable thing to have done?'

'Not in the panic I was in,' said Sidney. 'I don't think it was.'

'I suggest the communicating door was closed.'

'I don't know. I don't remember closing the door.'

The cross-examination carried on in that vein. Jowitt suggested he had placed the pillow on the pedestal after smothering her, then taken out his mother's false teeth and put them in the basin instead of in the glass because he was in a panic. Rosaline had been sitting dressed by the fire when he left her and, by his own admission, saw her for the last time, but her dresses were found hanging up on the back of the door. Sidney said he had helped her off with them, which he often did. He had not said so earlier because it was embarrassing and such an intimate thing to do.

'Did you tell the coroner that you had had a boxing match because you were apprehensive lest some bruise should be discovered on your mother?'

'Certainly not,' Sidney said indignantly. 'It was friendly play. I held her hands and then let go.'

'Is the truth about these insurance policies that you were desperately hard up for money?'

'I do not agree,' came his reply.

Sidney added that they had furniture stored in London. It was established that the storage charges were seven pounds, which considerably exceeded the value of the furniture. Sidney disagreed and said that it seemed rather a lot. The Attorney General cut to the chase.

'Mrs Morse had gone to Australia, and you wanted to go to Australia?'

'I did not want to go to Australia, and I would not have gone in my mother's lifetime.'

It was the truth, but Jowitt was determined to impress on the jury how Sidney consistently lied. Sidney said he lied simply to impress people. Jowitt called a prison officer into court and asked Sidney if he recalled, on his arrival in Maidstone, telling the officer he was a medical student. Sidney had described himself as a medical student before when he was on remand for the Rugby Mansions robbery. The jury of course knew nothing about that.

Jowitt now introduced the French newspaper, despite nothing of the sort being produced in evidence. Sidney said his mother had possessed a couple of circulars about motor coaches which had been given to her in France and which she had kept in her bag.

'Does it strike you as an extraordinary coincidence that a month later there should be found, among the charred paper, some French paper?'

'If it was a French newspaper, I cannot account for it being there.'

'Did you destroy your mother on the night of the 23rd of October in order that you might reap three thousand pounds from these insurance policies?' Jowitt put his final question.

'Most certainly not,' answered Sidney. 'It is a horrible suggestion. Horrible!'

After a brief re-examination by Mr Cassels, Sidney was touched lightly on the arm by a warder and with a slight smile on his face, maybe one of relief, he walked with quick, firm steps back to the dock. He had been in the witness box almost six hours.

A familiar and welcome face appeared in his stead, that of Pridie Sinclair. The elderly widow described the games she had seen Sidney play with his mother over the seven months they had lodged with her. They might well be described as 'sham fights'. They played 'all sorts of games', she said. They were both very affectionate. Her evidence was backed up by that of another landlady, Mrs Denton in Holloway, who said Sidney used to play with Rosaline but was never rough. She had seen him get hold of her shoulders and pat her cheek. She was in no doubt they were a devoted couple.

It was Professor Sydney Smith's turn to appear for the defence. There was nothing playful about Jowitt's approach. He went in for the kill. Smith affirmed his earlier findings. The bruise on the larynx, which had mysteriously disappeared, was in his opinion no more than a post-mortem stain. It was not an easy thing to distinguish with the naked eye and often impossible after putrefaction had set in. He trained assistants to be careful when making such observations, he said. He had seen no trace of bruising on the thyroid gland. There existed a few stray red blood corpuscles that had no connection with violence. Most telling was the fact that the hyoid bone wasn't broken, nor were there any traces of violence on the tissues under the skin or any of the ordinary signs of asphyxia in the internal organs. Professor Smith emphasised his very long experience in cases involving manual strangulation in Egypt.

'There is usually no delicacy in the touch of a murderer,' he summed up. 'He is always violent. He would move rapidly. He would want to get his victim killed at the earliest possible moment.'

'Among your cases, were there ever instances of strangulation by a young man of an old woman as she lay in bed?' asked Jowitt.

'I have had many cases of strangulation of elderly men and elderly women.'

'Will you try to answer my question.'

Smith thought about it and at length said, 'Yes I have had.'

'Do you mean to tell us you had not considered that question before you came to give evidence in this court?'

Jowitt continued to belittle Professor Smith. He read out a passage from *Taylor's Medical Jurisprudence*, a respected publication, on the title page of which Smith's name appeared as current editor. It seemed to conflict with his evidence in court about the signs of asphyxia. Smith denied that it did.

'I take it you have brought your notes of a person being strangled in bed?'

'No, I have not.'

'Was there one case or more than one case?'

'I have had many cases of a somewhat similar nature. May I explain?'

Jowitt wasn't going to let the professor explain anything.

'Please answer my question. It may be difficult for a gentleman who gives lectures to answer questions, but I want you to answer mine.'

'I am, to the best of my ability,' Smith replied, angry at the insult, 'but you won't give me an opportunity of putting you right. When I begin to explain, you say please answer my question. It makes it very difficult.'

There followed a duel about the half-crown bruise.

'You said that in training assistants you had to be careful in distinguishing between bruises and discolouration marks in post-mortem examinations. Do you put Sir Bernard Spilsbury on a par with one of your assistants?'

'Nobody can tell just by looking.'

Smith refused to denigrate his colleague, no matter how much he disagreed with him. 'I do not think anyone should say a bruise is a bruise until it has been proved that it is.'

'If you saw a fellow with a black eye, would you say let me put it under a microscope before I say it is a black eye?'

The question surprised Smith. It was not one he expected of the Attorney General. Jowitt did not wait for the answer.

'Sir Bernard says there can be no two opinions about it.'

'It is very obvious there can be,' Smith counteracted.

'You are bound to accept the evidence of the man who saw the bruise?'

'I do not think so.'

'How can you say there was not a bruise there?'

'Because if there was a bruise there it should be there now. It should be there for ever. The larynx is there to be examined by anybody.'

Dr Bronte fared no better under Jowitt's relentless cross-examination. He believed that Rosaline Fox had died of heart failure. There was enough disease, in his opinion, to account for it. As for the pillow, he could not conceive how it would not be stained by mucus and froth if it had been used for smothering.

On the half-crown bruise, Jowitt put to Bronte, 'Are you saying Sir Bernard did not see what he said he saw?'

In his thick Irish brogue, Bronte answered bravely, 'Far be it from me to make such a suggestion.'

Thirty years later, Smith would write of his absolute certainty that Jowitt personally wanted Sidney hanged. By that time, Spilsbury would be dead. The Fox case remained the most controversial of his career. It is still controversial today. But in Lewes in 1930, Spilsbury's opinion held sway, though not everyone in court felt entirely comfortable at the way the medical evidence was handled. One of those was Adelaide Foster.

Cassels attempted to steady the waters in his closing speech.

'No-one can claim for anybody infallibility. In my opinion, that bruise has been getting a place far too high, much higher than it really deserves, in the case for the prosecution…in a case of this kind, you are treading upon ground which is very dangerous.'

The danger for Cassels was that he could hardly expect the jury to give a lesser place to both Spilsbury's bruise *and* the insurance policies when they eventually took everything into consideration. They were the only real planks of the prosecution case.

The Attorney General departed the court after lunch and did not return. He left the final speech to his fellow prosecutor Sir Henry Curtis Bennett, who told the jury to do their duty and not to be afraid of finding the defendant guilty. If Spilsbury's infallibility and honour needed any more underscoring, Sir Henry was ready to provide it.

Referring to the bruise, he said, 'Sir Bernard Spilsbury had no doubt whatever that it was a bruise. Can you imagine that with the responsibility he has on his shoulders he could say that this was a bruise if there was any shadow of doubt about it? Do you think that with all his experience, Sir Bernard would have mistaken a post-mortem change for a bruise?'

At times, it almost sounded as though the prosecution were trying to convince themselves. Mr Justice Rowlatt summed up the case with reasonable fairness, scoring every point in Sidney's favour and pointing out the uncertainties where they existed, but he too reminded the jury of the eminence of the great pathologist. Nevertheless, he thought the fact that the brittle hyoid bone in the throat, which was unbroken, was a very strong point in favour of the accused. In spite of Sir Bernard Spilsbury's positive assertion on every single detail, the case was one of 'slight symptoms and obscure causes'. He asked the jury to consider very carefully the absence of any bruises or external marking on the body.

Just after 1.00pm, he sent them out to consider their verdict. After an hour and ten minutes, they sent for

Rosaline's set of false teeth. They returned at 2.43pm. It was Friday, 21 March.

They found Sidney guilty of murder. Mr Justice Rowlatt looked strained and emotional. The scholarly judge, who was far from being a hanger and a flogger like some of his compatriots, put on the black cap and pronounced the sentence of death by hanging.

'My Lord, I never murdered my mother,' cried Sidney.

Immediately a woman at the back of the court stood up and shouted, 'His own mother would forgive him!'

It was reported that as he was led from the dock, tears rolled down his cheeks.

Sidney did not appeal against the verdict, although Hindle made every effort to try to get him to change his mind. It is believed that he was the first convicted murderer sentenced to death not to do so. Had he appealed, it would almost certainly have been refused because of his homosexuality and the suspicions held by the police that he had tried to murder Charlotte Morse in spite of there being no evidence in that case. The dark forces in play would never have permitted a man like that to walk free or have his sentence commuted to life imprisonment. It is unclear if Sidney realised that.

The *Daily Telegraph*, commenting on the end of the trial, remarked, 'What spur is there so great, ask the chorus in the Greek tragedy, as to compel a son to matricide? The spur in these days apparently need be nothing more than a dissipated youth's craving for money when in dire need of it. How Fox can have supposed the insurance companies would not suspect so timely an accident on the very point of expiry of the policy is beyond understanding.'

It was beyond most peoples' understanding, but then most people didn't understand Sidney. The *Telegraph* was his favourite paper. He claimed it gave the most accurate report of his trial. One wonders what he would have thought of it comparing his life erroneously to the Greek tragedy of Oedipus Rex by Sophocles, in which Oedipus commits patricide, not matricide. Oedipus marries his mother. The chorus, the general public, nevertheless saw his refusal to appeal as an admission of guilt.

More likely, Sidney just wanted to get it over with. He had nothing left to live for. His best friend, his constant companion, was dead. She wasn't coming back for him. Ever, not ever. Only one person now remained to fight his corner, a sole voice in the wings.

* * * * * *

CHAPTER TWENTY-THREE

ADELAIDE FOSTER'S THIRTEENTH HOUR

On the day that Sidney was returned to Maidstone Prison and put into the death cell, Adelaide Foster went home and set fire to her carpet. Or rather, tried to set fire to her carpet.

What her husband Alfred, whose father was a police inspector, thought about this audacious act she didn't say, but she was determined to write to the Home Office and give her opinion on a trial in which she believed every single doubt had been unfairly weighted against Sidney, including the evidence of the fire.

Her carpet was similar in make to a Wilton, just like the one in Room 66, and she used a copy of the *Evening Standard* just as Rosaline might have been holding and reading it, with five sheets doubled over and one opened out. The flame burned the opened-out page rapidly until it reached the five sheets which were doubled. They fell to the floor and, lying flat, burned more slowly. There was no scorch mark on her carpet for about eight inches from the source of the fire, leaving a bridge of unburnt pile, which was exactly what had happened in the hotel room, and upon which the prosecution had based the case that the fire could not have been accidental.

Furthermore, she thought the experiments conducted by the 'experts' crude and futile. They had screwed up sheets of newspaper to try and create an accidental fire, but if it had been an accident, you did not get a number of sheets crumpled up. You only did that if you wanted to deliberately start a fire, which is what they believed Sidney had done. The fire chief, she reminded the Home Office, with all his years of experience, had been happy to tell the inquest it was accidental.

After offering to repeat her own experiments if they so desired, she laid into Spilsbury and the bruise. Spilsbury, she said, had gone to Great Fransham to see if there was evidence of foul play, the only reason he had been sent there.

'He sees this mark which he describes as a bruise,' she wrote. 'He is an expert pathologist. That was emphasised over and over again in the judge's summing-up. That bruise with all that depended on it, the life of a human being, was not preserved. It disappeared overnight and none of the other three experts were ever able to see it.'

Adelaide visited Sidney in the death cell and told him what she had done. She wasn't trying to have his sentence commuted to life imprisonment, she was determined to go all out for a retrial, and she firmly believed that in marshalling the evidence as she did, she stood a chance against the combined forces of the Home Office and the judiciary. Her experience with the Philip

Yale Drew case in Reading had taught her that there could always be an eleventh hour and one should never give up hope.

Sidney had convinced her, if she needed convincing, of his complete innocence. Why he didn't want to appeal, which any normal man would do facing execution, even if guilty, perplexed her. There is little doubt he captivated her as he captivated many men and women. She might even have been a little bit in love with him. In her letter, she would refer to him simply as 'her friend'.

Over the next two Sundays, Sidney's 'life story' appeared, such as it was, in the *News of the World,* and was picked up too in Australia. Given by him probably in return for help with his defence costs, the first part was headed 'Swindler and Thief—But I Did Not Kill.' He moralised about the snares behind the bright lights of London to which he had fallen prey, and made no secret of his frauds and prison sentences. It is full of repentance, almost painfully so, a warning to other young men not to follow in his path. The second part portrayed him as a lover of actresses, chorus girls and an admirer of one 'Miss Spitfire', a Soho denizen who thrashed a boxing champion in a night club. The various men in his life were merely friends who were good to him and helped him out when he needed it. Mrs Morse, too, was just a friend without whom he did not know what he would have done. His only love was for his mother, and one didn't need to read between the lines to get that.

It is reasonable to believe that Adelaide Foster was behind his story. After every visit, she went straight to the newspapers. Prison records reveal that she visited him practically every day after the trial and so was in a good position to get to know him. The sensational aspects blended with the fiction of a red-blooded heterosexual young charmer certainly reads like journalese, and there was potential for a novel in it. Adelaide would go on to write a number of novels, one of which was about—no surprises—a feisty female journalist.

Her letter to the Home Office, comprising seventeen typewritten pages, landed on the desk of the Secretary of State, Mr J.R. Clynes. It remains in the case files with a hastily scribbled note on the back saying that every point had been dealt with and pressed upon the jury and that there was no need to refer her letter to the judge.

For Adelaide Foster, there was to be no eleventh hour and no thirteenth hour either. She had done all she could. Stories now leaked out to the newspapers about the gas tap incident in Southsea, stories without any corroboration which painted a picture of a young man who had attempted murder before. The first appeared in the *Daily Telegraph* and was picked up on the other side of the world in the *Melbourne Argus* of 31 March, eight days before Sidney went to the gallows and at a time when the Australian readership were keen to lap up any information on Charlotte Morse's amorous adventures in the mother country.

Meanwhile Sidney kept himself busy writing letters, many of them replies to members of the public who had supported him, others to his relations and friends. To Pridie Sinclair on 6 April, he wrote:

'My darling Pridie, my dear friend, I am afraid there is no hope now. I was informed yesterday that the

Home Office saw no reason to interfere. Do not grieve, dear one. I just want you to know that my thoughts are with you, and I thank God for giving me such a friend. Apart from any action which you have done, your letters with their inspiring messages of comfort have done so much to help me. I thank you, darling Pridie, my heart is too full to say all I want to. Think of me dear, as I know you will, of one who loved and cared for his dearest mother. I go to my end an innocent man, but this makes it so easy if it means I am to meet mother and your dear self again one day; then how happy I am to die. Yes, very happy.'

He sent his best wishes to members of her family and the friends he made in Shenfield, a time that he obviously cherished.

'I have not been feeling too fit,' he continued. 'The strain of the past few weeks has been just a little too much, and at times I know I am almost on the verge of collapse. I have not one single thought of ill will towards anyone. It is just a terrible mistake, but I had hoped that things would have been righted before it was too late. Well dear Pridie, I cannot write more. I wish you a final goodbye. Think of me sometimes. My best wishes for you and may you be restored to health and spend many happy days to come. Bless you Pridie for the wonderful soul that you are. Yours, Sidney.'

To his cousin Mrs Gaynor in Holloway, he expressed the wish that his mother's gold watch be given to her.

In spite of Sidney's wish that there should be no reprieve, attempts were made. There was a growing movement within the legal profession against capital punishment, and in 1928 a bill by Lieutenant Commander the Honorary J.M. Kenworth, MP, passed its first reading by just one vote, only to be knocked into the long grass by the then Home Secretary Joynson Hicks who was firmly against abolition. The National Council for Abolition of the Death Penalty only a month before Sidney's trial had presented a petition with more than four times as many signatures as previous ones.

A number of cases gave fuel to their cause. In Arizona, Eva Duggan, a housekeeper found guilty of the murder of an elderly man, had just become the first woman to hang in the state. As her body was launched through the trap door, she was horribly and crudely decapitated in front of witnesses, many of whom collapsed at the sight. In Germany, while Sidney was sitting in the condemned cell, a farm labourer, who had been sentenced to death for strangling his sweetheart, had it commuted to two years imprisonment when medical witnesses agreed that he had merely shaken her violently and that she had died from heart failure, a case that bore some similarity to Sidney's. But it was the Scottish case of Oscar Slater which preyed on so many consciences. For the murder of a woman, Marion Gilchrist, in her home in Glasgow, the Jewish bookmaker had been sentenced to death, but that sentence was commuted to life imprisonment. After spending two decades in prison, during which time new evidence was amassed and books written about his case, one by Sir Arthur Conan Doyle, his sentence was finally quashed.

The clumsily named Mission of Intercession, South London and Croydon, had started to become vocal about cases of capital punishment, and had already protested against Norman Thorne being hanged after being found guilty at Lewes Crown Court of the chicken farm murder. Now they turned their attention to Sidney, presenting a petition to the Home Office and saying that if the sentence was carried out, they would arrange for a service outside the prison gates. The Mission were not entirely against the death penalty, just its nature. Five years earlier, they had forwarded a resolution for a Royal Commission suggesting that a 'lethal chamber' should be substituted. One can only assume that none of its members had actually witnessed a death in the gas chamber in the United States.

The day before his execution was due to take place, Sidney's solicitor announced that no representation would be made to the Home Office on the grounds of insanity. Sidney himself had expressed his extreme disapproval of any idea of putting forward such a plea, even one that broached upon his epilepsy. Sidney had no desire to live the rest of his life locked up among the mentally ill and the criminally insane.

By a stroke of irony, on the same day, Captain Morse's suit was held in London before Mr Justice Hill in the Divorce Court. Sidney was probably not even aware, and besides, he had more important things to think about. Charlotte's friends, the Weston sisters, gave evidence of the adultery they had witnessed at Southsea, and an employee of the Strand Hotel told of the nights Sidney and Charlotte had spent in three different rooms. The divorce was granted. Sidney thus made history again by being the first convicted murderer to be cited as co-respondent while under sentence of death.

Among Sidney's last visits was one from Lady Theodosia Bagot, to whom he had written a letter. Dosia was Sir John Leslie's daughter whom Sidney had known at Manchester Square when he was a page boy.

Like her father, she had taken an interest in the cherubic lad who once charmed the family. She must have wondered what they would have thought now. But here she was, to close the circle, to see him again for herself before he died. Although she retained her title, Lady Bagot had remarried the Reverend Sidney Swann, a famous sporting parson whose memorable exploits included cycling round Syria and riding from Land's End to John O'Groats. She and Sidney would have had much to talk about.

Controversially, her nephew Shane Leslie, the Leslies' grandson, would write in the sixties that while to the prison chaplain Sidney was obdurate, Dosia, who was religious and was the founder of the Church Army, had softened him up so much that Sidney was prevailed upon to confess to her. It is strange therefore that on 13 April 1930, Mr Leslie, the 'well known author' said nothing about the confession in a piece he wrote for the *Weekly Dispatch,* five days after his execution. There is no evidence that Sidney confessed to anyone. In fact he appears to have protested to the end that he would go to his death an innocent man. The story must therefore be taken with a few pinches of salt, particularly as Leslie devotes only eight lines to it in his memoir and cuts a long story so short he can't even be bothered mentioning the actual crime.

On the day of the execution, Sidney rose to meet his fate. The *Dundee Evening Telegraph*, a newspaper which followed murder cases closely, headed its story in bold capitals 'A DANDY TO THE END'. He dressed in the smart tailor-made blue lounge suit which he had worn at the trial. It was the prison chaplain Eric Dawson's first experience of an execution. Not so

Robert Baxter, the executioner, who had served as assistant to Albert Pierrepoint and was regarded as a quiet, efficient and sober man.

Sidney ate his breakfast and spent about an hour with Dawson. He was said in the press to have swayed as he walked to the gallows and had to be assisted, but as with Dosia's visit, a convict's last moments are often coloured. At 8.15am, he fell through the trap door of the newly built gallows. Death was instantaneous due to fracture and complete dislocation of the neck. Five minutes later, a warder emerged and nailed on the door the Sheriff's declaration that the penalty had been paid. No bell was tolled, no flag was raised, and inside, routine went on as usual. In line with procedure, Sidney's body was buried within the prison precincts.

Soon after, his waxwork effigy made its appearance in the Chamber of Horrors at Madame Tussauds. The company acquired a suit he had once worn. It was retrieved from a bag in one of the hotels which Sidney had quickly left without paying the bill, and the hotel insisted Madame Tussauds pay the outstanding amount before using the suit in the exhibition. The *Daily Sketch* reported that the first morning the wax Sidney was on display, a visitor cut off all the buttons and a cheap tie-pin was also purloined. More black buttons were sown on, but they too disappeared. A reporter who examined the suit described it as being cheap and off-the-peg. There were no tailors' bills in the pockets. Even his Eton tie caused controversy. A visitor who had attended Eton complained, and the tie was removed. In time, so was Sidney.

The only person who knew the truth about what happened in Room 66 of the Metropole Hotel on that night in October had gone to his end. For all the statements taken, all the words spoken at trial, all the experiments made, how Rosaline Fox met hers remained a mystery.

Within days of the execution, William Fox lost his job at the Alexandra Hospital. It was not unconnected with his brother's crime, even though he had an exemplary record. During the trial he had been demoted to orderly, with a reduced salary, which he reluctantly accepted, but the publicity was too much for the hospital authorities, who finally terminated his employment. His young wife died only a few months later. William remarried, took over a pub in Portsmouth, and died in 1957. Rosaline's only granddaughter, Marjorie Fox, married a French polisher Reginald Maddox and moved to Brighton. Ordinary life went on.

* * * * * *

CHAPTER TWENTY-FOUR

SIDNEY FOX'S CRIME

A British trial is an adversarial procedure. While we may like to believe that it always arrives at the truth, it often does not. Opposing sides battle to get their version of events over the net, and a jury of twelve has to decide who they believe. Had Sidney's trial taken place in Scotland, a verdict of Not Proven would have been an option. Not so in England. The jury in Sidney's case had to decide which of four medical men with opposing theories to believe, and to base their judgement on that.

Prejudice no doubt played an important part. Sidney was a fraudster and a liar and a thief. He had therefore to be a murderer. If you believed the prosecution's version of events, he took poor Rosaline out of the workhouse and towed her around the country with thousands of pounds of insurance policies in his pocket in order to kill her so that he could live in the style he coveted. What happened in Margate was not an accident. It was a carefully arranged plan. The only mystery was why he took so long to bring it to fruition.

2007 saw the publication of Andrew Rose's long-awaited and excellent book on Sir Bernard Spilsbury, *Lethal Witness*. It is a thorough examination of all Spilsbury's famous and not-so-famous cases. At the same time, it is a biography of a haunted man who, after a lifetime of service, committed suicide by turning on the gas in his laboratory, an action that could have caused a major explosion and killed others. He was lonely and depressed, with health and money worries, and saw no other way out. His abilities were declining, and he was probably aware of that fact. Younger men were coming onto the scene and for him work was drying up. Sixteen years after the Fox case, he gave evidence in his last murder, in which it was obvious to colleagues that he was no longer the confident and persuasive individual he had once been.

Not for Spilsbury was it enough to reflect on past glories, on his reputation as the man who had dragged forensic pathology out of the dark ages and made it his speciality, becoming a media star into the bargain. He was a household name. He had been lifted onto a pedestal by a public who worshipped him for his cool professionalism and apparent infallibility. He sent murderers to the gallows. A man with such an awesome responsibility could not possibly be mistaken, and if he was, surely he would admit to that. Wouldn't he?

Today, most people would be hard-pressed to think of the name of any pathologist. Murderers become the celebrities, their victims are quickly forgotten, and the expert witnesses pass through the courts, their names largely ignored by the general public. We are more knowledgeable of programmes like CSI, where entertainment meets science and makes it look exact, just as Spilsbury liked juries to view his evidence. No obfuscation, no doubts, just certainty. One imagines Spilsbury would have heartily approved of the programme. Scientists made gods. Forensics stripped away of its mystique. Spilsbury liked to talk in language that the layman understood, not scientific gobbledygook. Simple images like a bruise, for instance. Everyone knew what a bruise was.

Rose does not shy away from suggesting that Spilsbury may have sent innocent men to the gallows or sent to the gallows men who might have been found not guilty had it not been for his lofty manner and unequivocal style while giving evidence. He made mistakes. He made assumptions. In the Crippen case, which partly depended on the identification of a body found in the cellar, believed to be that of Crippen's wife, he found what he recognised as a scar. Crippen's wife, Cora, had recently been operated upon. Two other experts believed it was merely a fold in the skin, not scar tissue at all. In the chicken farm murder, Norman Thorne described himself as a 'martyr to Spilsburyism' after the great man said what other experts called skin creases were marks of hanging. Thorne may possibly have been the victim of a miscarriage of justice, though other evidence, including his dismemberment of the body afterwards and hasty burial, rather told against him. We shall never know. In his chapter on Sidney Fox, Rose expresses unease at the verdict based on the bruise that 'disappeared' and rightly suggests that Spilsbury was not only just mistaken and incapable of admitting he might have been wrong, but by the time of the trial he crossed into the dangerous territory of perjury.

I shall go a considerable step further than that.

A few years ago, I wrote a stage play based on the Fox case, based on my own research in the files held at the National Archives, during the production of which I reached that same conclusion. I read every statement, perused every document, over a period of many days. It was the fact that no one ever saw Sidney harm so much as a hair of his mother's head that impressed me. They seemed to be good pals, just as Sidney said they were. I had intended taking it to the Edinburgh Fringe in 2020 when Covid struck. Amanda Bailey, an actor I had worked with in Edinburgh on my previous production, *The Good Scout*, suggested performing it on Zoom. She assembled a cast of three who would perform while seated from the isolation of their own homes. Sidney was played by Sebastian Calver, a young man I had met at his drama school showcase a year previously. James Dale Cassels was played by Mike Duran. Amanda herself took the role of Rosaline Fox. It was well received, and Amanda and Sebastian set up a beautifully tender and playful relationship as mother and son.

When things returned to near normal, and theatre audiences started coming back, I seized the opportunity to produce *Sidney Fox's Crime* on the stage in the 100-seat Above The Stag Theatre in Vauxhall, south London. Amanda and Sebastian once again played Rosaline and Sidney. This time J.D. Cassels was played by Mark Curry, of *Blue Peter* fame. Mark had recently come out of *Wicked*, in which he starred as the wizard, and wanted to cut his teeth on grittier theatre. He was thrilled at the opportunity to play a barrister trying against the odds to save his client from the hangman's rope. The play was set in Sidney's cell, in which Cassels takes him through the story of his life, interspersed with flashbacks to his life with Rosaline, leading up to the climax in the Margate hotel.

Before rehearsals began, I took Amanda and Sebastian on a 'field trip' to Norfolk so they could see the village where Sidney grew up and went to school and where Sir Bernard Spilsbury performed his autopsy. I had been there before, of course, but for my actors it was their first time. It was one thing to read about the case in the evidence, quite another to see the place. Great Fransham is way off the beaten track. You think you must have passed it until you suddenly come across the long, low single-storey building on which there is still a plaque that reads Great Fransham Village School. It was locked up and in the process of being redecorated, but it was possible to look through the window and see the small room with an open door at the far end. This was where Spilsbury found the infamous bruise on Rosaline's larynx. There must have been numerous police officers sitting around idly in what is now used as a village hall. He would have had no problem in putting his head out of the door and asking someone such as Inspector Hambrook to verify his findings. They were less than a few feet away, but as we have seen, as he preferred to do, Spilsbury worked alone in that small room at the end of the gloomy schoolhouse. I do not know what the light was like that November afternoon, but he must have been doing the job as quickly as possible so the body could be placed back in the coffin and returned to the ground.

As I had done on a previous visit, we searched for Rosaline's grave, but it was unmarked, though we identified the corner of the quiet churchyard in which it must have lain, next to her parents. Across the field was the small labourer's cottage in which Sidney and his brothers grew up, and a short distance along the road was what remains of Great Fransham station. Part of the platform has been neatly preserved, but it is now a private home. From here, Rosaline took her two lovers from the railway. There cannot have been much privacy in Great Fransham.

For Amanda and Sebastian, the trip to Sidney's birthplace was invaluable. While rehearsing the play, they weren't just reading dialogue, they were visualising as they spoke. In their very first scene together, Rosaline packs Sidney off to school with a kiss on his cheek. She tells him she is meeting someone off the train. Sidney asks saucily if it is a gentleman she is meeting, and she tells him it is none of his business. It is the first time we see a bond develop between them, a cheeky playfulness and a physicality that would develop throughout the play.

No one, of course, can now know how Sidney and his mother really behaved together. The actors developed their roles based on all of the evidence. But it was by that process and through directing them that I began to guess at a solution to the mystery. There was no way I could leave a burning question mark at the end of the play. It would have been very unsatisfying for the audience and something of a cop-out for me. I wanted to propose a theory, to present an interpretation of what I thought might have happened in Room 66 that night. Amanda and Sebastian, too, had to find the truth in their own performances. They had built up such a lovely affectionate and mischievous relationship that for Sebastian to suddenly turn on his mother and strangle her to death was not only unthinkable to me but also to him. It was completely out of character. As actors sometimes will put it, 'What's my motivation?'

In real life, as in drama, one also needs motivation. I do not pretend that a play can get at the truth, in the same way that this book can only be an attempt to find the answer, but both have helped me to try and get inside the heads of Sidney and Rosaline Fox.

I believe the key to the mystery lies in that trip to Belgium and France to visit Cecil's grave. It was something Rosaline had always wanted to do. Having accomplished that, they returned to England, to their round of defrauding hotels by not paying their bills. Virtually penniless and with little more than the clothes they wore, they must have known their time was running out like sand through an hourglass. It was only a matter of time before they would be arrested. Sidney would return to prison, and Rosaline would once again be taken into the workhouse. She knew she was not well. It is not too hard to believe that the last months of her life were an opportunity for Sidney not to murder her but to give her the pleasure of staying in fine hotels, living like a lady, eating fine meals in good restaurants. He had waited a long time, years in fact, to take her abroad and make her dream come true. To have arranged her death on such an occasion would have been not only cruel but purposeless. He wished her to enjoy her last days. There were so many other insured days, about six months' worth of them, in which to seize that final, brutal opportunity. They were in no hurry to start with, but it needed to happen before the police tracked them down and took it away from them. The possibility of that happening sooner rather than later was heightened in Canterbury when Sidney, about to leave without paying the bill, was dragged back to face the manager and threatened with the police.

An anonymous letter sent to the Home Office after the trial began by inviting the question, 'Has it occurred to no one that Mrs Fox might have been responsible for what her son is about to be hanged for?'

The notion that Rosaline had suicide in mind is not far-fetched. If it was to happen, she needed Sidney to help her. What did they discuss in these dark hours, this odd pair, their lives so locked together they could not tear themselves apart? Her final gift to Sidney would be the money to set him up for life. But it had to be quick and painless. They had eaten a good dinner that night. Afterwards, the half-bottle of port which Sidney went out and bought certainly helped.

Spilsbury almost unwittingly set the scene himself by telling the court that the absence of bruising on the neck could be accounted for by the victim *offering very little resistance*. The Attorney General also ventured down that path by supposing she was asleep and *depressed by port*. The woman in court who shouted at the end of the trial that his own mother would forgive him saw that possibility.

I would suggest that they did it before Sidney came back down to the bar for his couple of drinks. She became drowsy after the port, and he put the pillow across her face, but she struggled in fear, and her heart gave out before the act of asphyxiation took place. Sidney panicked. His mother was dead. He still had to make it look like an accident. The policy lasted until midnight. He had time to think. He *needed* to think. He came back down to the bar and went upstairs again at 10.40pm, not with murder in his heart, but a plan to create a fire and fill the room with smoke. He was calm now, methodical. He was careful not to make too much of a fire but just to let it smoulder so the atmosphere in the room thickened until he could hardly breathe or see his mother. He undressed as though for bed, to make it look as though he had been sleeping, then made the mistake of shutting the door to preserve the scene and rushed downstairs.

The pillow, which became so big a part of the prosecution case, was never examined. No one noticed if it had froth or mucus on it. It may have, it may not. Perhaps Rosaline's heart gave out before there was time for anything to stain the pillow. That would fit the evidence, confirming the findings of Professor Smith and Dr Bronte that she had died of heart failure, not asphyxiation.

As for Sidney's hands round Rosaline's throat, he had never shown her violence, nor was he clever enough to strangle her and leave no marks. A pillow was soft. He did not have to look at her. She did not have to look at him. When we enacted that scenario at the end of the play, it was disturbing to watch, and Sebastian's cries of 'Mother!' when he realised the deed was done were all too real. It was a measure of their acting that audiences found it chilling to watch.

Which leaves us with Spilsbury's bruise. In the week before we opened, the BBC television programme *Murder, Mystery and my Family*, which resurrected old cases and retried them along with the participation of a descendant of one of the parties, featured the Fox case. Helping the two lawyers was a young woman called Laura Chandler-Page (no relation) who was descended from one of Rosaline's brothers. Laura had already concluded that Sidney was not guilty, and the legal experts on the programme certainly branded the verdict unsafe, saying that Spilsbury's evidence would never have been allowed today, let alone be such a major pillar of the prosecution case.

It is now generally believed that Smith and Bronte were right and Spilsbury was wrong. I will go that step further into Rose's dangerous territory of perjury and cross right through it. I believe the great pathologist lied, not just to himself, but deliberately, under oath, in a courtroom. As such, it was unforgivable. It is unforgivable now.

He had been called by the police to conduct an autopsy on an exhumed body, to search for signs of foul play. On the drive north and over breakfast in Cambridge, he learned from Inspector Hambrook that Rosaline's son had insured her life and that she had died minutes before the policy expired. Spilsbury knew the stakes were high and had probably already made up his mind that this was murder, or at least that it was a very suspicious case. Hambrook would not have lost the opportunity to tell Spilsbury that Sidney was openly homosexual, had slept with famous men for money, that he had been a fraudster all his life. Such a man needed to be taken out of society.

Eleven days after Spilsbury examined the body, Hambrook asked the Portsmouth police to investigate the gassing incident at Southsea. No doubt the two mates discussed the findings, or rather the lack of them. It was another eighteen days before Spilsbury finally filed his report. Had he nothing to include that would bolster the prosecution case, his standing would have been severely tarnished. His job was to help the police, not to look for anything that might aid the defence. Frustration would have set in; he would have gone back to his laboratory and left the police baffled. A wicked man would have gone free. Spilsbury *had* to find something, even if it wasn't there.

'*What would Spilsbury find?*'

The bruise that wasn't there served its purpose, and Hambrook's devil incarnate was taken out of the world.

I contacted the producers of the *Murder, Mystery and my Family* television programme and invited Laura along to the opening night of the show. She found it an intriguing experience and spent a long time afterwards talking to the actors who had played members of her ancestral family. Laura had researched the case herself, though she hadn't gone so far as to sift through the case files in the National Archives as I had. Nevertheless, she still believed Sidney was not guilty of Rosaline's murder, not even as assisted suicide, which of course was still murder in the eyes of the law. I respect that view. I would not be so dogmatic as Spilsbury and say there can be no two opinions about it because there are. Of course, readers will have their own.

With that, I am inclined to rest my case.

* * * * * *

THE END

SOURCES AND ACKNOWLEDGEMENTS

The National Archives at Kew contain a number of voluminous and very fat files on the Fox case, and I used these extensively. MEPO 3/862 contains the Metropolitan Police Files, while the five HO 144/11767–11771 boxes of Home Office Registered Papers contain all of the available witness statements of friends, family, landladies, hotel staff and many others who came into contact with the Foxes. PCOM 9/280 has the prison commission papers, including Adelaide Foster's written submission.

Sidney's 'Royal Flying Corps' credentials, such as they were, can be found in MH106/2203/174, Folios 360–361, dated 17 Oct–7 Nov 1917.

The newspapers covered his case extensively, and I have used, with caution, his own very self-serving 'life story' as published in the *News of the World* prior to his execution. The British Newspaper Archive has been invaluable, as has TROVE, the Australian press archives regarding the Morse saga. I would also like to thank the Norfolk Record Office for their help in researching the Foxes and, in particular, Sidney's school records. The

City of Westminster Archives aided my research into Gerald Hamilton's younger years.

Of the books I have referred to, *The Trial of Sidney Harry Fox*, edited by F. Tennyson Jesse in the Notable British Trials series, referred to in the text, has been the most valuable. As we have seen, Miss Tennyson Jesse was able to talk directly to a number of the protagonists, now long dead, while Andrew Rose's *Lethal Witness* (2007) contains a very incisive account of the great pathologist Sir Bernard Spilsbury's involvement with the case.

Others were *Some Were Spies* (1955) by Earl Jowitt, Sidney's avowed prosecutor, which contains a revealing chapter on his case, as does *Hambrook of the Yard* (1937) by Walter Hambrook, the detective in charge. Both these sources indicate strongly what the feeling was towards Sidney Harry Fox at the time by his prosecutors, or maybe one should say persecutors. *The Man who was Norris* by Tom Cullen sheds much light on Gerald Hamilton, Sidney's first 'mentor', along with Hamilton's own autobiographical offerings.

Sir Sydney Smith's *Mostly Murder* (1959) gives the other side of the forensic case, while Shane Leslie's *Long Shadow* (1955) was used for background about the Leslie family of Manchester Square. Richard Whittington-Egan's book *The Ordeal of Philip Yale Drew* was most helpful regarding Adelaide Foster's role in this story. Richard, now sadly departed, was a good friend of long standing and encouraged me greatly in criminal byways.

At the time of writing, Margate Museum, which has been very helpful, are participating with me on the production of two performances of *Sidney Fox's Crime* within the setting of the very Magistrates Court in which Sidney appeared. I would like to thank the trustees of the museum, particularly Robin Haddon, and its dedicated volunteers.

Everything else, including the history of the Foxes in Norfolk, and Rosaline's six-year relationship with James Nelson from Necton, is old-fashioned genealogy involving vital documents, press reports, case files, censuses and wills. By such means, I have also unearthed much new material, including Sidney's association with Walter Tarrant and the 'Raffles' hotel thefts.

An immense debt of gratitude is owed to Benoit Paturel, John Owen and Above The Stag Theatre in Vauxhall, south London, the only full-time LGBT theatre in the country, who gave me the opportunity to stage *Sidney Fox's Crime* as part of their final season of plays. At the time of writing, the venue is now closed, but it is hoped that the theatre will find another home in the not-too-distant future. My thanks also to Amanda Bailey, Mike Duran, Mark Curry and Sebastian Calver, who brought Sidney and his world to life for me. Their contribution was a revelation. Lindsay Siviter was extremely helpful to me in unearthing facts about Sidney's later appearance in the Chamber of Horrors at Madame Tussauds and material regarding Sir Bernard Spilsbury. As always, Stewart Evans was ready to assist with material from his vast crime collection. Christopher Delaney, my partner, who read every word of the manuscript and spent many hours, days and months living with Sidney Fox as I did, deserves wholehearted thanks. Throughout the dark days of Covid and the lockdowns, he never tired of being a sounding board for my obsession with the case.

Finally, I have tried to find something good in Sidney, almost a thankless task as he has been given a rough ride by most writers. He wasn't an angel, far from it, but neither was he, as Detective Inspector Hambrook believed, the devil himself. There were a lot of devils in the case of Sidney Harry Fox, but there were good people too, who tried to see justice done and who looked for the light in the darkness.

Glenn Chandler

* * * * * *

INDEX